# City Ghosts

# City Ghosts

## True Tales of Hauntings in America's Cities

Sterling Publishing
New York

Published by Sterling Publishing Co., Inc.
387 Park Avenue South, New York, NY 10016



Distributed in Canada by Sterling Publishing
c/o Canadian Manda Group, 165 Dufferin Street,
Toronto, Ontario, Canada M6K 3H6

Distributed in the United Kingdom by GMC Distribution Services,
Castle Place, 166 High Street, Lewes, East Sussex, England BN7 1XU

Distributed in Australia by Capricorn Link (Australia) Pty. Ltd.
P.O. Box 704, Windsor, NSW 2756, Australia

ISBN-13: 978-1-4027-3539-4
ISBN-10: 1-4027-3539-1

Printed in the United States of America


2 4 6 8 10 9 7 5 3 1

# Table of Contents

# Introduction

What are ghosts? No one knows for certain. Many experts believe that ghosts are people who are trapped in a place that they formerly inhabited—be it a home, a workplace, or a locale where the deceased person has intense emotional memories. Some say that ghosts are popular in our culture only because everybody enjoys a good scary story; others assert that belief in the existence of spirits reassures us of a never-ending existence.

*City Ghosts* is a guide to ghosts and hauntings in cities throughout the United States. Each chapter focuses on an area of the country and the different haunted experiences that our cities have to offer, bringing together some of the nation's spookiest places—where ghostly presences are felt, and where, sometimes, things actually do go "bump in the night."

Some humorous, some haunting, and some just late-night terrifying, these stories span our rich cultural heritage, from the earliest settlers through the Civil War times to modern day tales of haunted buildings.

The aim: to help the reader feel and gauge the presence of spirits in public buildings, city mansions, cemeteries, and places likely or not in major cities across the country. We bring to life the stories of unusual activity in the hopes that, ultimately, the reader can put himself or herself in the role of psychic or volunteer paranormal investigator looking for signs of the netherworld.

We have also included information about ghost tours and contacts to the places where the legends of ghosts have made them famous, making the book almost a travel guide for ghost aficionados.

# The Northeast

From the Boston waterfront to the White House, ghostly citizens haunt the historically-rich cities of the East Coast.

From the Boston Common to the cobblestone streets of Philadelphia to the boroughs of New York City and the grand parks of Washington, D.C., you will find some of the famous and not-so-famous ghosts that haunt the cities of the Northeast.

While walking through the streets of Philadelphia, you may encounter the ghosts of our founding fathers; at Boston's harbor, Lewis Wharf will surprise you with spirited fun; and New York City has so many ghost stories that even the most ambitious ghost hunters cannot keep track.

Find out why Washington, D.C.'s Lafayette Square is one of the nation's capital's most haunted spots and why Dolley Madison is still a well-traveled first lady.

In Baltimore, Edgar Allan Poe still resides as a ghostly resident, and, while you're there, visit The Cat's Eye Pub for an old-fashioned drink with an old-fashioned ghost.

The older cities of the East offer many chilling, strange, and sometimes disturbing encounters based on historical events and unusual haunted experiences.

# Boston, Massachusetts

The Boston Tea Party, the Boston Massacre, the Old North Church and Paul Revere's ride. Home to some of the most important events in the history of our young republic, Boston today is the capital of New England and one of our most important cities. Stroll the old historic streets of Boston, and your companions might just be of the ghostly persuasion. The eeriness of the dark streets and historic architecture will keep you stepping lively as you explore the city of extraordinary normal and paranormal activity.

## Spirits Stroll through Boston Common

Dating back to 1634, Boston Common is one of the oldest public spaces in the United States. The land was purchased by the townspeople of Boston to serve as a militia training field and for the feeding of cattle. Much of the Common was used as a public livestock grazing area, and it also served as a public green. But, a section of it was used as a burial ground.

The Central Burying Ground, located on the south side of Boston Common, near Boylston Street, is the one of the nation's oldest burial grounds. The earliest burials here were likely those of poor people. The graves' occupants include Native Americans, murderers, thieves, witches, pirates and others deemed "undesirable" by the Puritan regime. Many convicted criminals were hung from the trees here, left to rot as an example to others. In fact, hangings here continued until 1817.

It is said that unmarked graves and the neglect of the dead often causes cemeteries to become haunted. And, the Central Burying Grounds is certainly haunted. Visitors to the old graveyard have encountered spirited mischief, being poked in the back, tapping on shoulders, keys and wallets being snatched—but not by a human force. Shadowy figures have been seen floating in the trees, perhaps a witch hung there so long ago.

Boston Common is a more than 50-acre park in the middle of downtown Boston. But, most everyone agrees there are ghosts on the green. The spot called London Green, where a seventeenth century mass grave was dug for victims of the "Black Death" is so unsettling few like to linger here; a great sadness overcomes you and the park's gardeners know that any flowers they plant here will not grow.

Near the Cherub that stands in the fountain at the Arlington Street entrance, two elderly ladies called "Proper Bostonians" dressed as if coming from a nineteenth century tea, stop passers-by and smile hello, and then vanish into thin air.

In fact, much of Boston Common has an undercurrent of grief and loss. You may feel the energy seeping out of you as you stroll in parts of this lovely park and gardens; be aware that many lost souls still wander the grounds.

BOSTON COMMON AND THE CENTRAL BURYING GROUND
BETWEEN BOYSTON, PARK, TREMONT, AND BEACON STREETS
Starting point of the Freedom Trail

## Phantom Sailors on Leave

Located in the North End, Lewis Wharf is the home of The Boston Sailing Center and an almost-hidden garden of lush flowers and herbs, a beautiful oasis in the bustling city. The Boston Harborwalk passes by this somewhat "secret garden" with a soothing fountain, making for a relaxing stop on your walking tour.

Lewis Wharf has many historical commercial and non-commercial buildings. There is an historical exhibit where you can check out the numerous historical photographs and artifacts collected from the area.

While on the Harborwalk, you will pass by the Pilot House, built in 1839 as a rooming house for pilots and captains of the ships spending the night in the Boston Harbor. The Pilot House has a restaurant on the first floor, where poltergeist activity has been experienced for years. A woman in white haunts the kitchen on the first floor, where doors slam shut by themselves. The murmurs of men talking and drinking, and glasses breaking as if thrown against a wall, are heard on the upper floors. There are the sounds of people coming and going in and out of the house, along with phantom laughing and noises on the stairs—only there is no one there. It would appear as if some of the present-day Pilot House occupants are not ready to head out to sea.

There have been apparitions of sailors and seamen at Lewis Wharf; when it is dark and misty, you might feel the presence of others, and see small rounded orbs floating above the water. Beware of ghosts looking for a companion.

LEWIS WHARF AND PILOT HOUSE
BOSTON'S NORTH END

Find out more about the Pilot House and Boston Harbor from
The Boston Harbor Association (Harborwalks)
374 Congress Street, Suite 609
Boston, Ma. 02219
617-482-1722
www.tbha.org
www.bostonharborwalk.com

## Former Hotelier and Host Continues to Haunt

*"Such guests!*
*What famous names its record boasts,*
*Whose owners wander in the mob of ghosts!"*
—Oliver Wendell Holmes, in his poem "At The Saturday Club"

In the heart of Boston, along the Freedom Trail, is the world-famous Omni Parker House, the oldest continuously open hotel in the United States. Founded in 1855, it has played host to many of the rich and famous. Literary greats like Emerson, Thoreau, Hawthorne, and Longfellow met regularly in their legendary nineteenth-century Saturday Club. Baseball greats like Babe Ruth and Ted Williams, along with politicos such as Boston mayor James Michael Curley, presidents Ulysses S. Grant, Franklin Delano Roosevelt, John F. Kennedy, and Bill Clinton, all frequented the hotel.

From its kitchen it has made American culinary culture, inventing the famous Parker House roll and Boston cream pie. The Parker House has been a training ground for internationally known chefs.

The Omni Parker House is close to Boston's theater district, and it has played an important role for thespians. Many of the finest actors of the nineteenth century made the hotel their home away from home, including Charlotte Cushman, Sarah Bernhardt, Edwin Booth, and his brother John Wilkes Booth, who was seen pistol practicing nearby only eight days before the assassination of Abraham Lincoln. During the twentieth century, stage, screen, and television stars, from Joan Crawford, Judy Garland, and William ("Hopalong Cassidy") Boyd, to Adam "Batman" West, Kelsey Grammer, and David Shiner, have made the Parker House their Boston home. Today, the 551-room Omni Parker House remains one of Boston's oldest and most elegant hotels.

It's also one of the most haunted. Employees have reported that there are several ghosts that inhabit this old hotel in the heart of downtown Boston. Doors open and close by themselves, lights mysteriously turn on and off, voices have also been heard throughout the night. Several employees have quit their jobs because they have been frightened by the lost souls who haunt the hotel.

The apparitions appear to be of older times based on the attire and hairstyles of an earlier, more aristocratic era. One of the ghosts is the hotel's founder, Henry D. Parker. To understand why Parker continues to haunt the hotel today, it is important to understand the depth of his commitment to this establishment. In1825, the 20-year-old farm boy arrived in Boston from Maine with less than one dollar in his pocket, and in immediate need of employment. His first job was as a caretaker for a horse and cow, a job that paid him eight dollars a month. Then, he became a coachman for a wealthy Watertown woman, and, after observing the finer material things, he was set on his career path.

By 1832, he had raised enough money to open a restaurant, which he called simply "Parker's." A combination of excellent food and service won over a regular clientele of businessmen, lawyers, and newspapermen. By 1854 he embarked on a larger dream—he decided to build a first-class hotel and restaurant.

Parker purchased the former Mico Mansion and razed it. In its place, Parker built an ornate, five-story, Italian-style stone and brick hotel, faced with gleaming white marble. The first and second floors featured arched windows, and marble steps led from the sidewalk to the marble foyer within. Once inside, thick carpets and fashionable horsehair divans completed an air of elegance. Above the front door, an engraved sign read simply "Parker's." Upon opening, it was recognized as one of the finest establishments of the day.

The hotel expanded again after Parker's death; in 1925, the original marble palace was torn down, and a more modern Parker House was erected-the one we know today, which was completed in 1927. One of the original wings remained open during construction, allowing the Parker House to maintain its designation as America's oldest operating hotel. The 1927 version is even more elegant than its predecessor.

The staff believes that Parker is attempting to keep things up to his high standards, monitoring activities while walking through the halls, sometimes by continually rearranging the furniture in the rooms. During recent construction work in the hotel, workers saw Parker wearing a hardhat as though inspecting the work. Certainly, Parker is continuing his lifetime quest for hospitality and is roaming the halls and the hotel restaurant to check on his guests.

OMNI PARKER HOUSE HOTEL
60 SCHOOL STREET
617-227-8600

## Some Love lasts a Lifetime, True Love lasts Forever

Fort Warren dominates the thirty-nine-acre island known as Georges Island, only seven miles from downtown Boston. The fort was built between 1833-1869. During the Civil War, it was used as a training facility for Union soldiers, and as a prison for Confederate soldiers.

Unfortunately, it became the last desperate scene of a Civil War Love Story. In June of 1861 a Confederate soldier, Andrew Lanier, was about to head into battle. He begged his commanding officer to allow him leave to propose and marry his true love. He was given a 48-hour leave, and he did marry and had a short but happy honeymoon. His wife was heartbroken when he had to return to his troops.

By the end of the summer, the young lieutenant was injured in battle, and, lying unconscious on the battlefield, he was taken prisoner and shipped off to Fort Warren. He succeeded in sending his wife a letter, telling her of his miserable accommodations in the "Corridor of Dungeons"—how horrible he felt, his fear that he would never get out alive, and his greatest heartbreak: never seeing her again. He gave her directions to come and find him.

His wife, a beautiful Georgian belle, decided that she could not wait for the inevitable letter to arrive, telling her that her husband was dead—she would take action. She devised a plan, cut her hair, acquired a pistol and a man's suit of clothing. She then convinced a blockade runner to take her to Boston Harbor.

Days later, the boat reached Hull, Massachusetts, and dressed like a young Yankee lad, Mrs. Lanier made her way to the home of Southern sympathizers. There, she was not far from Fort Warren, and she studied the fort through binoculars while on the beach. She soon learned the routines of the fort, when guards changed, where the barracks were, and where the prisoners were held.

On the moonless, stormy night of January 12, 1862, she decided to make her move. She had someone row her to the island, carrying her pistol and a pickax, and dressed as a man, she left the boat. She timed her moves so she could sneak pass the sentries as they marched in opposite directions. She scrambled over the wall and fell into the prison's parade yard. She soon found the "Corridor of Dungeons" and marching up and down the rows of prison cells, she quietly whistled one of their favorite songs. At first, there was no response, so she whistled louder and finally heard the needed reply. She was whisked up and pulled through the Dungeon's narrow bars—being petite and wet helped. She was soon in her husband's arms.

The Confederate soldiers were already planning an escape, but they now had a pickax. They decided to dig a tunnel toward the parade ground and the arsenal, then armed, overtake the Union guards.

The tunnel took weeks to dig but they finally broke through, only to be met by Union soldiers who had heard the noise. They were all captured; the escape plan failed. Lanier and his wife had stayed back, waiting to go out once the guards had been overtaken, but they were soon confronted by the guards. Mrs. Lanier pulled out her pistol, pointed it at the head of the nearest soldier, and demanded all of the guards to surrender. The guards' commander quickly moved forward, and grabbed for the gun. However, she took a wild shot, hitting her husband in the head. He died instantly.

He was buried in an unmarked grave with no ceremony. She was declared a spy, and an order for her immediate execution was given. Her death by hanging was set for the next day.

Her last wish was to not be dressed as a man, but as a woman. They found an old black robe, and she draped it over herself. She was hung and buried next to her husband. The date was February 2, 1862.

Just a few weeks later, the first sighting of Mrs. Lanier, "The Lady in Black," began. A sentry on duty felt invisible hands around his neck, choking him, and then he saw Mrs. Lanier starring at him. He ran away as if his life depended on it and refused to do guard duty at night again.

Over the years, the other sightings included finding small, lady-like footprints in the snow, when no women were stationed at the fort. Soldiers would collapse, feeling as if they are being choked near the spot where she was hung. She has often tapped people on the shoulder, and then a blast of chilling air hits the person in the face when they turn around. She has been seen on the grounds in her black robe, a shadowy cloaked figure walking the island. There are on record court-martial cases of men who shot at her ghost-like figure while on sentry duty.

Therefore, when you visit Fort Warren, now a National Historic Landmark, open to the public from May to Mid-October, let yourself imagine the courage and love that turned a Southern belle into a female adventurer in men's clothing, determined to rescue her husband, the love of her life.

FORT WARREN
GEORGES ISLAND PARK
Now serves as the entrance to the Boston Harbor
Island State Parks
www.bostonislands.org

# New York City

New York City is the largest, noisiest, and busiest city in the United States. But, New York is not only our most populated city with living beings, it's also the home to many to a large number of our formerly departed.

## Aaron Burr Leads the Spooks of New York City

There are many ghosts and spirits found in New York City, especially in Greenwich Village, one of New York's oldest neighborhoods, and a popular spirit hangout.

The restaurant, One If By Land, Two If By Sea, is the popular haunt of Aaron Burr, former U.S. Vice President, who, these days, is primarily known for killing Alexander Hamilton in a duel in 1804.

The restaurant's ambience is romantic, with lovely piano music providing the backdrop to a dining experience reminiscent of another age. But, some unsuspecting patrons have encountered the angry spirit of Aaron Burr, who is said to move chairs out from under guests, bump waiters serving trays, sending food and dishes crashing, send a chilly air around the dining room, and create havoc with the fire in the fireplace.

Once a carriage house owned and operated by Burr, the Greenwich Village restaurant is also said to be haunted by Burr's daughter, Theodosia Burr Alston. As Burr's only child, she and her father were devoted to each other, and Theodosia was a source of great comfort to Burr during his long 1807 trial for treason, for which he was finally acquitted.

Apparitions of Theodosia in a flowing white dress have been seen floating throughout the restaurant. She supposedly adored beautiful jewelry and loved earrings that glittered; women sitting at the bar have remarked that they feel something, or someone, tugging on their earrings.

Theodosia lived in the Carolinas with her husband, wealthy plantation owner Joseph Alston, with whom she had a son, Aaron Burr Alston. After the death of her son from tropical fever at the tender age of ten, her father convinced her to come to New York. Her ship, the *Patriot*, vanished without a trace off the coast of the Carolinas on December 30, 1812. Some speculate that she and her ship fell victim to coastal pirates.

There are also reports of Theodosia's ghost in the same flowing white dress being seen hovering over the water on the beach of Huntington State Park in South Carolina.

## ONE IF BY LAND, TWO IF BY SEA
## 17 BARROW STREET

## All in the Family

The Burr father and daughter duo are not the only ones whose spirits have come back to clear up unfinished business. At The Morris-Jumel Mansion, in the section of Manhattan now known as Washington Heights, Eliza Jumel, the ex-wife of Aaron Burr and former mistress of the mansion, is said to wander around the house in a purple dress, making rapping noises on the walls and windows. She and her first husband, Stephen Jumel, a wealthy wine merchant, restored the mansion in 1810.

A British Colonel, Roger Morris, built the mansion in 1765. George Washington had his headquarters here during the Long Island Campaign of the Revolutionary War. Today, the mansion serves as a popular museum and tour destination.

A popular story about the mansion is that of a history teacher, taking her class for a visit, entered into a room and a Revolutionary War soldier appeared, as if he just stepped out of a painting on the wall. She fainted on the spot. Other visitors have seen the soldier as well.

Eliza's first husband, Stephen Jumel, was said to be a very upset and angry ghost. No one ever saw him, but visitors and employees talk about being pushed from behind, and having a feeling of dread. He was also known for throwing objects at people. A rumor that his wife murdered him was proven true when the famous ghost hunter Hans Holzer and a medium, Ethel Myers, conducted seances in the hopes of freeing his angry spirit. They were successful: it was true that his wife had murdered him. She had let him bleed to death after an accident; in fact, she had even removed his bandages. After the truth about his earthly departure was out, his spirit stopped haunting the mansion.

The servants' quarters, which were located on the top floor, is frequented by the ghost of a young servant girl who committed suicide by jumping out of a window, a victim of a tragic love affair. Her apparition is still seen wandering in that area.

Visitors to the mansion, which is said to be the oldest home in Manhattan, also report meeting the ghost of Aaron Burr, who was Eliza's second husband. After a year as a widow, Eliza married the disgraced former vice president in the mansion's octagonal parlor in 1833. A year later, she filed for divorce against Burr, saying he squandered her money on Texas land developments and committed adultery. The divorce became final on the day of Burr's death at age 78 in 1836.

THE MORRIS-JUMEL MANSION
65 JUMEL TERRACE
WASHINGTON HEIGHTS

## There's No Business Like Show Business: Theater People are Still Making Appearances

The ghost of Aaron Burr also appears at the very southern tip of Manhattan, looking out to sea. He seems to be waiting for the ship that Theodosia sailed on, which never arrives.

St Paul's Chapel, at Broadway and Fulton Street in Lower Manhattan, was built in 1766, and many of the famous and not-so-famous have worshipped here. George Washington attended a service here on his Inauguration Day. A headless actor, George Frederick Cooke, haunts the church's small graveyard. He was a slightly-known British actor who bequeathed his head to medical science to pay off debts. When he died, his head was removed. Rumor has it that it was used in a Shakespearean production of *Hamlet* before it was returned to the medical school. Cooke died in 1812, and in 1821, fellow thespian Edmund Kean erected a monument to his memory, for Kean considered Cooke to be the world's finest actor. Now, Cooke's headless ghost is seen in the graveyard, particularly around the monument. He also roams the streets near St. Paul. Encountering his apparition can be extremely disconcerting, as any headless person would be.

A quick stroll to the magnificent Trinity Church at Broadway and Wall Street may net you a visit by Alexander Hamilton, who was buried here after his duel with Aaron Burr. He haunts the graveyard, his sad ghostly shape in the clothing he died in floating among the tombstones. Another less sad spirit, that of comedian Adam Allyn, has been known to make strange laughing noises; some visitors to the graveyard tell of creepy laughter coming from his grave.

New York City has many a haunted theater—from the tiny Cherry Lane Theater on Commerce Street, where, once again, Aaron Burr, who lived nearby, is seen in the hallway near the dressing rooms; to the New Amsterdam Theater on 42nd Street, which is haunted by a chorus girl; to Radio City Music Hall, where a glamorous couple dressed formally in 1930s attire have been seen. They are thought to be the Hall's builder S.L. "Roxy" Rothafel and his girlfriend, catching one more opening performance. David Belasco is still associated at least in spirit to the theater that bears his name on West 44th Street.

He has been seen often in what looks like a religious-style choir robe wandering the upper floors of the theater; since his death in 1931, usually at least one person will see him on a new play's opening night. He quickly vanishes when spotted.

Many of the New York theaters that have ghosts report the same type of activity. The most common activities are props being moved or hidden, lights going on and off, elevators moving when no one is around, curtains being pulled, ghost-like figures sitting in seats, apparitions standing to the side of the stage, and spirits walking through walls.

One of the most haunted New York theaters is the Palace Theater, built in 1912. Shortly after it opened, a theater manager named "George" hung himself from a fly door, now near the fly door is a very strong smell of cigarettes. George was never without his Old Holborns, and to this day, he is still lighting up. The Orchestra pit has had a ghostly piano player, when no one is seen pressing the keys. Sometimes a cellist in a flowing white gowns plays along with the phantom piano player. Many, many ghosts have been reported over the years at The Palace Theater, perhaps because of the many different acts that played here—from music revues, dramatic plays, operas, big bands, and vaudeville acts.

One of the Palace's ghosts is that of Louis Borsalino, an acrobat and tight robe walker who fell to his death from the high wire. He broke his neck, and his terrified screams as he fell and the horrific impact of his body hitting the stage can still be heard occasionally by actors and crew as the stage is being set for a production. Louis is not willing to be forgotten by the stage that took his life. The experience is very upsetting to those who have heard it and it is said that if you hear him falling and see his ghostly spirit on the way down you will also have an unfortunate accident. Obviously, this is theater lore, but it all has some foundation in reality.

Another famous and recognizable ghost has appeared near an

orchestra door that was made specifically for her when she was "playing The Palace." She is seen peaking out the door, but she quickly vanishes. Those who have seen her say just one look and you know you have just seen Judy Garland.

The Palace Theater has been renovated and is the theater for the musical production of Anne Rice's *Lestat;* her celebrated literary vampire appears on stage along with the other restless spirits.

THE PALACE THEATRE
1564 BROADWAY (between 46th and 47th Streets)

There are many, many ghosts and ghostly locations in New York City. There are the ghosts of Peter Stuyvesant in St. Mark's Church on East 10th Street, Edgar Allan Poe in a former home on West 3rd Street, and the Astor Library Ghost. If haunted houses, parks, historical taverns, speakeasies, or haunted houses interest you, you can take one of the tours.

Haunted and Mysterious New York
www.newyorktalksandwalks.com
New York City Cultural Walking Tours
www.NYCwalk.com

## A Tree Grows in Brooklyn

"Frances thought it was the most beautiful of churches in Brooklyn. It was made of old gray stone and had twin spires that rose cleanly into the sky, high above the tallest tenements, inside, the high vaulted ceilings, narrow deep set stained-glass windows and elaborately carved altars made it a miniature cathedral."

—Betty Smith, A Tree Grows in Brooklyn
(New York, Harper & Brothers, 1943)

Betty Smith, originally Elizabeth Lillian Wehner, was baptized in the Holy Trinity Roman Catholic Church on January 24, 1897. Her famous novel, about growing up in Williamsburg, Brooklyn, describes the now Most Holy Trinity Roman Catholic Church

The church is one of the most beautiful structures in New York City. The church on Montrose Avenue, designed by the church architect William Schickel and built under the guidance of Father John Stephen Raffeiner, was completed in 1885. The glorious towers were added in 1890. The church owned the whole block, and there are many false doors and closets leading to an underground tunnel system under the church. And, the church's school is built on top of an old cemetery.

If you walk around the church, especially near an outside staircase that leads to the basement, you will feel very cold and a sense that you are not alone. Footsteps can be heard but no one is there. Dogs will stand at the top of the stairs and growl for no apparent reason. Lights in the school gym flicker on and off.

In the area around the church, you may feel as if you are being watched, and a feeling of fear can overcome you. When the church was built, it took years of grueling work from many of the immigrants who passed through Williamsburg. Many an accidental death occurred and perhaps their collective energy has somehow stayed close to the church.

MOST HOLY TRINITY ROMAN CATHOLIC CHURCH
MONTROSE AVENUE, WIULLIAMSBURG
BROOKLYN

## Spirits Haunt Historic Neighborhood for More Than One Hundred Years

Although Staten Island is one of the boroughs of New York City, for most of its history, it has been a rural community, where farming and local tradesmen lived, worked, and thrived. And Richmond Town was a hub of the local activity.

There are many historic buildings in Richmond Town, and you can take a very informative daytime tour. Included in the tour of the historic structures and houses are the Historic Museum; the Third County Courthouse; and Voorlezer's House, a National Landmark building (ca. 1695) that is the oldest schoolhouse in New York.

Voorlezer's House is also haunted: many photographers have noted that pictures taken around the building have numerous orbs in them.

It is the same for the old courthouse; there is an orb that lingers around the witness stand inside the courthouse. The small graveyard next to the old courthouse has many a restless spirit. The one seen most often is a young girl, anxiously looking for a lost love, sometimes mistaking living young men for him. She will approach the young men only to fade away quickly when she realizes that he is not her one true love.

There are other haunted places on Staten Island: Fort Wadsworth, where soldier ghosts play games with visitors; Wolf Pond Park, the site of the murder of several children in the late 1970s, apparently the deeds of a serial murderer who was never caught; and St Augustine's Monastery, where the spirit of a monk who went insane and murdered everyone present now roams the halls. Researchers say his presence is particularly strong in the sublevels.

These are just a few of the many haunted spots on Staten Island, known for being so close but so far from Manhattan.

HISTORIC RICHMOND TOWN
441 CLARKE AVENUE
STATEN ISLAND, NEW YORK

# Philadelphia

Known as the City of Brotherly Love, Philadelphia was the crucial location in the founding of our American Republic. No city has a greater claim to being the birthplace of our nation—the Declaration of Independence was written and adopted by the Continental Congress here; the Liberty Bell was rung at the first public reading of the Declaration on July 8, 1776; during the Revolution the encampment at Valley Forge was just a few miles outside the city; after the War for Independence was won, the Constitutional Convention took place here; and, of course, Philadelphia was the hometown of Benjamin Franklin, one of our most important early citizens.

## You Never Walk Alone in the Old City

But, Philadelphia is also the home of many ghosts, with some of the founders of our nation still hanging around. There are some who say that even Benjamin Franklin can be seen in the older parts of town.

Philip Syng Physick was one of the world's foremost physicians, who became known as the "Father of American Surgery." He now haunts his former home, a beautiful house with period furnishings, on South Fourth Street.

Samuel Powel was the last mayor of Philadelphia under the crown, and the first under the new Republic. Known as the "Patriot Mayor," he's been seen in his old home on South 3rd Street.

There are reports of ghostly apparitions and the sound of mysterious footsteps at the Betsy Ross House on Arch Street in Old City Philadelphia.

Benjamin Rush was one of the signers of the Declaration of Independence; he was the U.S. Surgeon General, and he became the Treasurer of the U.S. Mint in 1799. These days, he is said to haunt his old house in Philadelphia. Visitors report seeing a cat sitting in the window, but no cat lives there.

Independence Hall, on Chestnut Street between 5th and 6th Streets, is where the Continental Congress met and where the Declaration of Independence was signed; it is said to be haunted by some of our forefathers, who still gather in the halls.

While in the city, you may decide to eat at the City Tavern, where a former waiter is always on the job. He still shows up, sometimes changing the place settings, moving the silverware around. The City Tavern, on Second Street at Walnut, is a restaurant where you can experience an authentic eighteenth century meal. And, it is not only authentic; it serves award-winning food.

OLD CITY PHILADELPHIA
OLD CITY CIVIC ASSOCIATION
9 NORTH 3rd STREET
215-440-7000

## My Country, Right or Wrong!

St. Peter's Church Cemetery on Fourth and Pine Streets has been home to ghosts for a long time. A phantom horse-drawn carriage has been seen charging through the center of the graveyard. There are other reports of restless Native American chiefs roaming the grounds.

My country, right or wrong! These often-quoted words were first said by Commodore Stephen Decatur, one of the most important naval officers in the history of the United States.

Commodore Decatur served his country in Tripoli against the Barbary pirates, in the War of 1812, and was U.S. Navy Commissioner from 1816 to 1820. Decatur was killed in a duel in 1820 by Commodore James Barron. He is now buried in the cemetery of St. Peter's Church, but his ghost has been known to wander around the cemetery. He is also said to haunt his last home in Washington, D.C.

The words that Decatur actually said are: "Our country! In her intercourse with foreign nations may she always be in the right; but our country, right or wrong."

ST. PETER'S CHURCH CEMETERY
FOURTH AND PINE STREETS

## The Ghosts Continue to Protect Our Waterways

Work on Fort Mifflin on the Delaware River was begun before the Revolution in 1772, but it was completed in 1776 by American Revolutionary forces. In 1777, when British General William Howe, with 20,000 troops occupied Philadelphia, he tried to capture Fort Mifflin so that he could get supply ships up the river and be able to pursue George Washington. Four hundred American soldiers held off over 2,000 British troops and 250 ships for several days. The patriots' stand allowed George Washington to retreat to Valley Forge.

During the Civil War, Fort Mifflin was used a prison for Confederate troops, as well as other prisoners. Some of these prisoners are still seen and heard from today.

Now, the fort has been restored and is open to the public for tours. These days, visitors to Fort Mifflin report seeing faces peering out windows from empty rooms, windows and doors open and close when there is nobody near, and there are a woman's screams late at night. And, even an occasional muffled gunshot. There is also a lamplighter who has been seen making the rounds at night in the empty fort.

FORT MIFFLIN
FORT MIFFLIN ROAD
ON THE DELAWARE RIVER

## Spooky Cellblock Continues to Haunt

Every Halloween, Eastern State Penitentiary, a grim former state prison on Fairmount Avenue, is the place to be for those looking for a ghostly time. Hundreds of people show up for the annual "Terror Behind the Walls" tour. The journeys through the haunted cells of this twelve-acre site are offered by candlelight, and are not recommended for the faint of heart.

These days, pained former prisoners are said to haunt its dark Gothic halls. Halloween visitors regularly report seeing the "Soap Lady" dressed in white in the last cell on the second floor. Other figures thought to be ghostly inmates from the prison's early days have been seen.

Indeed, the huge stone prison, with its solitary-confinement cells and thirty-foot-high walls, is allegedly teeming with caged spirits who are, after many years of confinement, anxious to get out. Watching over these imprisoned spirits is the apparition of a guard, who has been seen in the prison's high guard tower late at night.

Eastern State Penitentiary was famous for being one of the most expensive buildings ever built in the United States when it was opened in 1836. The prison was thought to be a new and novel design in prisons and inmate treatment. Architect John Haviland designed this landmark experiment in architecture and building technology to embody the latest ideas about institutional reform, civic responsibility, and criminal behavior. Its model became the blueprint for many prisons around the world.

The unique construction was built with a central hub with hallways extending from it. This required fewer guards, since they could keep an eye on all the hallways and cellblocks from one central location. The prisoners were kept isolated. Each cell had its own feed door and exercise yard, which prisoners were allowed to use for only one hour a day. There was no communication with the guards or with other prisoners. Whenever prisoners were allowed to leave their cells, they were forced to wear hoods over their heads.

The penitentiary was designated a National Historic Landmark by the federal government in 1965. It is now open for historic tours.

EASTERN STATE PENINTENTIARY
2124 FAIRMOUNT AVENUE

# Baltimore, Maryland

Baltimore was founded in the seventeenth century as a commercial port on the upper Chesapeake Bay. The present city dates from July 30, 1729, and is named after Lord Baltimore, the Proprietary Governor of the Province of Maryland. Baltimore rapidly developed as a seafaring and trading community. Baltimore has been called "Charm City" because of the quality of life this pristine harbor city offers its residents, whether they are living there now or are there only in spirit.

Melissa and Amy from Fell's Point Ghost Tours shared their stories of the Cat's Eye Pub and Duda's Tavern.

## Some Cats Have Nine Lives

In 1726, William Fell purchased the waterfront land that today is known as Fell's Point. Over the years it has served as Baltimore's main port and shipyard. Many a seaman and working man looked to the local bars for drinks, good stories, and female companionship.

One such establishment is The Cat's Eye Pub, which is in the building of a former brothel. When the pub was renovated not too long ago, it was discovered that numerous red light switches were hidden in the walls. This was common: the use of the "Red Light" on or off switch would indicate if a "lady" was available. It is said that some of the spirits of the "ladies" still haunt the building, and loud clicking noises are heard in the walls even though the light switches are covered up.

These days, the Cat's Eye is a well-known live music venue in Fell's Point. The Cat's Eye also has a reputation for practical jokes and strange antics; its one-time owner, Kenny, and Jeff, a long time bartender, established the humorous antics. Although Kenny and Jeff are no longer part of the living world, their spirits also linger at the pub they so loved. The Cat's Eye has a photo gallery displayed on one of the walls. Pictures of them and other regulars proudly overlook the pub, all but one pictured on the wall are dead. Thus, they can watch over the patrons and keep the pranks coming

Kenny and Jeff loved publicity, and liked nothing more than to get their names in the newspaper. One of the ways they tried to accomplish this was that they would design elaborate pranks. One of their more well-documented escapades was to stage a New Orleans style funeral for a member of the IRA. They claimed that the deceased was in a coffin, and with musical accompaniment, marched the coffin down the street. The police waited for them at The Cat's Eye, since carrying a dead body in public is against the law. However, just as they were going to put an end to the spectacle, Kenny jumped out of the coffin.

Jeff, who some said had more than a passing resemblance to Abraham Lincoln, loved to dress up (Cupid was a favorite) and his favorite shirt was emblazoned with his drink of choice (Vodka Tonic No Fruit) with a red circle and slash through the fruit.

Now the spirits of Kenny and Jeff mingle with the liquid spirits; they have been known to knock items off the walls, move things around, and try to help the staff with the financial books. Needless to say, the help is not always welcome.

Melissa, one of the owners of the Original Fell's Point Ghost Walk, has this story to tell. One morning she stopped by the bar and the bar was empty except for the bartender. He talked her into buying a T-Shirt. They talked for about fifteen minutes before she left, not thinking that anything was out of the ordinary. Melissa and Amy, the other owner of the tour, returned about two years later to do research for the Ghost Walk. While speaking with some of the female bartenders, Melissa happened to ask them about the bartender who sold her the T-shirt. They asked what time of day it was when she made the purchase. She replied that it was fairly early in the morning, not too long after the bar had opened. They looked a bit surprised and asked Melissa to describe the man who sold her the T-shirt. She said he looked sort of like Abraham Lincoln, tall and thin. The shocked look on their faces told Melissa that something was not quite right. One of them said, "There was a bartender, who fits that description, and he worked here on the morning shift for thirty years, but he died eight years ago!" She pointed to a photo hanging on the wall behind the bar. Sure enough, it was the man who sold Melissa the t-shirt!

A tradition of paying tribute to those who have passed on is very much in the culture of The Cat's Eye staff and patrons. Nowadays, they hold a yearly pub-crawl for Jeff.

THE CAT'S EYE PUB
1730 THAMES STREET

## One More Polka

Duda's Tavern, a Fell's Point restaurant and tavern, was built in the 1850s as the Union Hotel. Thirty years later, it became the Maryland Bay Pilots Association and was a Seamen's rooming house. It became a tavern after Prohibition; the current co-owner John Flury's in-laws bought it in 1949.

Duda's proudly displays a sign that hangs outside proclaiming "fine foods and spirits;" the spirits are certainly plentiful and the food is very fine. There are also ghosts everywhere: upstairs, in the Tavern, and down in the basement. Employees and tenants all talk about seeing floating ghosts, and a recent bartender talks about seeing a man with "curly black hair, white trousers, and an old-time, navy-blue sailor top with gold buttons." When this bartender looked at him more closely, the sailor quickly disappeared, seemingly into thin air.

Footsteps can be heard upstairs when no one is up there. In the basement, an older man wearing a flannel shirt and suspenders appears and then vaporizes. He also enjoys tapping unsuspecting employees on the back, scaring them back upstairs.

There is one particular ghost that has inspired many stories. His name was Doc and he was a merchant seaman who lived upstairs for years and years. He was a very gentle, well-liked man, and was known as being very friendly to the workers from the nearby canning factories. He also enjoyed the company of the college students who frequented the Fell's Point bars. One art student went so far as drawing Doc's portrait on an index card, which Doc treasured and displayed behind the bar.

Doc had a great fondness for a particular obscure polka song, and only he played it on the Tavern's jukebox. Patrons knew they would have to tolerate the playing of Doc's song, especially as the night wore on and the beer was flowing. This went on for many years and most of the people who frequented Duda's were amused, and laughed at the first-timers who would regard the jukebox with a mixture of astonishment and annoyance when the polka rang out repeatedly.

Doc passed away in 1980, and the polka record was removed from the jukebox. After his death, the owners of the bar had him cremated, since they had never heard Doc speak about any family. The owners planned to scatter his ashes in the Chesapeake Bay where he liked to fish when they went vacationing at the beach with a group of friends. One day, a woman they had never met approached them; she was the girlfriend of their beer distributor, and she asked them if they had a person's ashes. They were understandably shocked and answered 'yes." It turned out that she was psychic and had a strong feeling that Doc did not want his ashes scattered. A few days later, a man showed up at Duda's asking about Doc. He turned out to be his brother; he had heard that Doc had passed away and wanted to bring his ashes back to be buried in their family plot.

Well, everyone thought that this last message from the grave was Doc's final farewell. However, on a weeknight not too much later, the regulars were sitting around the bar when suddenly the jukebox began to play Doc's polka. They all felt their hair stand on end, and they sat there, stunned. After the song finished, they checked the jukebox for the record, but it was not on the machine. Doc had said goodbye the best way he knew how, by playing his song one last time.

If you go to Duda's, take note of the curved corners outside. Superstitious sailors thought that evil spirits gathered in sharp corners; therefore, this building was built with no sharp corners. If you eat there, the crab cakes are recommended.

DUDA'S TAVERN
THAMES AND BOND STREETS

FELL'S POINT GHOST TOURS
Co-Owners: Amy Lynwander & Melissa Rowell
http://www.fellspointghost.com
Tours run March-November

## The Poe House is Haunted by a Grandmotherly Spirit

Since he died on October 7, 1849, the living have kept the famous writer's spirit alive, but Edgar Allan Poe himself also is alive, as a ghost. Apparitions are said to haunt Baltimore's Edgar Allan Poe House, which was built around 1830 in what was then the country. Poe's Aunt Maria Clemm rented it in 1832. Poe lived there with his grandmother, aunt, and two cousins until 1835. Virginia Clemm, who later became his wife, was one of the cousins living there.

In the 1930s the Poe House was scheduled for demolition, but public interest forced the housing authority to spare the site. The Edgar Allan Poe Society was given control of the house, and it was restored and opened as The Baltimore Edgar Allan Poe House in 1949, one hundred years after his death. An exhaustive search of city registers, deeds, and maps proved that Poe in fact did live in this house in the 1830s. The Commission for Historic and Architectural Preservation (CHAP) now maintains the site as a historic house museum, and sponsors tours and activities throughout the year.

Many of the curators of the museum and neighbors report seeing a candle-like light that goes from floor to floor when the museum is closed at night. Doors and windows open and close by themselves, and an apparition of an old heavy set women in 1830s-style clothing has been seen in the upstairs bedroom, where Poe's grandmother died.

In 1836, Poe married his 13-year-old cousin, Virginia. Poe was devoted to his wife. When she finally died a tragic death from consumption in 1847, a painting of her was done from her corpse and hangs in the museum. The picture has a very eerie feeling as you walk by it. Poe outlived her by only two years; the cause of his death remains a mystery.

Each year at Halloween a special ceremony is held at Poe House to honor Poe, and it is said his spirit is always felt during the event.

Poe was born in Boston on January 19, 1809; he was the grandson of a Baltimore Revolutionary War patriot, David Poe, Sr. He was orphaned at three, but raised by Mr. and Mrs. John Allan in Richmond, Virginia. It is said that Edgar was never fully accepted by Allan and the two had a strained relationship.

Many of Poe's works have a death theme, and both the modern detective story and the modern horror novel trace their roots to him.

Poe rests with his wife and aunt under the monument erected to him at Baltimore's Westminster Graveyard. Each year for more than half a century, a mysterious black-clad stranger makes a pilgrimage to the grave of Edgar Allan Poe, leaving behind three roses and a bottle of French cognac. Wearing a black hat, black overcoat, and white scarf, he appears in the early hours of the morning every January 19th to toast the writer on his birthday. The identity of the visitor is not generally known. A crowd usually gathers outside the brick wall to catch a glimpse of the visitor.

EDGAR ALLAN POE HOUSE & MUSEUM
203 AMITY STREET
BALTIMORE

# Washington, D.C.

Washington, D.C., is our nation's capital city, and the heart of our government and its leaders are located here. Some of our former leaders are still in town, but now many as ghosts.

## The Adams Family

Lafayette Square, where the rich and the powerful built their beautiful stately mansions, is a seven-acre public park located directly north of the White House on H Street between 15th and 17th Streets, NW. The Square and the surrounding structures were designated a National Historic Landmark District in 1970. Originally part of the grounds of the White House, it was called "President's Park;" it was separated from the White House grounds in 1804. In 1824, the Square was named in honor of General Lafayette of France.

The Hay-Adams Hotel on Lafayette Square was built in 1927 on the site of Henry Adams's mansion, which had been built in the 1880s. The ghost of "Clover" Adams, Marian Hooper Adams, haunts this stately hotel. Clover is the wife of Presidential Advisor Henry Adams, who is a member of the famous Adams family of Boston; Henry is the grandson of John Quincy Adams, sixth President of the United States.

Clover was well read and extremely bright, and their home soon became the literary salon center for Washington's intellectual elite. Clover, who had been nicknamed by her father, was also a photographer.

She did suffer from depression, and after her father's death, she began to spend more and more time alone, sitting for hours staring into the fireplace in the apartment. One day, Henry came home to find Clover unconscious by the fireplace, a bottle of potassium cyanide by her side. The belief was that she had used the chemical from her photography to take her life. Henry's beautiful, brilliant wife was dead.

These days, Clover's ghostly floating figure has been seen throughout the Hay-Adams Hotel. The smell of mimosa is in the air on the hotel's eighth floor. A sixth-floor housekeeping closet will never stay locked, and staff have reported seeing Mrs. Adams hovering around the door. In 1997, all the doors of the second floor guest rooms opened at once, causing the head of security great angst. They have attributed these occurrences to the presence of the ghost of Marian Hooper Adams.

Marian Hooper Adams is buried in Washington's Rock Creek Cemetery; her tombstone is that of a hooded woman designed by Augustus Saint-Gaudens. This statue is called "Grief," and it is said that anyone standing in front of it will begin to cry and feel a great sense of loss.

HAY-ADAMS HOTEL
ONE LAFAYETTE SQUARE

ROCK CREEK CEMETERY
CHURCH ROAD & WEBSTER

## The General Daniel Edgar Sickles and Philip Key Deadly Encounter

General Daniel Edgar Sickles, held many impressive positions in his long life—assistant to President James Buchanan, U.S. Congressman from New York, a Commanding General in the Union Army, and an Ambassador to Spain. He was also a womanizer and murderer.

In the 1850s, Sickles married a beautiful young woman, Teresa Bagioli. Around the same time, he became good friends with Philip Key, a Washington D.C. lawyer and son of Francis Scott Key, the composer of "The Star Spangled Banner." Key was a widower with four children to raise on his own. His uncle was the Attorney General of the United States.

Daniel Edgar Sickles adored prostitutes and was unwilling to give them up. Philip Key often filled in for Sickles with his beautiful wife Teresa, escorting her to the theater, often dining with her at the Sickles home. And, Sickles was often absent, his time taken up with politics, work, and carousing.

The relationship between Teresa and the handsome, attentive Philip Key soon developed into a full blown love affair. Key went so far as to rent an apartment near the Sickles residence at Lafayette Square. He devised a way to signal Teresa that she should come over by hanging a string from his upstairs apartment window.

While Washington's upper crust had ignored the behavior of Sickles, the openness and brazenness of Teresa and Philip's affair became the talk of the town. Daniel Sickles received an anonymous letter hinting that Key and his wife shared more than a platonic friendship, giving some details about the Lafayette Square apartment. Sickles immediately confronted his wife, who denied the story. He believed her, at least for the time being—he could not imagine his best friend and his wife betraying him so.

But, Sickles could not ignore the gossip; he decided to take action. The day was February 27, 1858; it was a clear, crisp Sunday afternoon when Sickles sought out Philip Key. He found him in Lafayette Square, and shot him three times.

Philip Key was dead, Sickles turned himself in, and the press had a field day with the sensational story of love, betrayal and murder. Sickles was the wronged husband. He had future Secretary of War, Edwin M. Stanton, as his lawyer, and he was acquitted. It was the first use of the temporary insanity defense in the United States.

Philip Key now haunts Lafayette Square, walking near Maynard House, the spot where Sickles shot him almost one hundred and fifty years ago.

When Daniel Sickles lost his leg at the Battle of Gettysburg, he donated it to the Smithsonian. The shattered leg sits under glass with a card "Compliments of General D.E.S." It is now part of the Walter Reed Army Medical Center's Visitors Center Exhibition. Sickles, however, is very attached to his leg and is said to haunt whatever spot where it is being showcased. His ghostly apparition has appeared in full uniform.

LAFAYETTE SQUARE
H STREET, BETWEEN 15th and 17th Streets, NW.

## Better Late than Never; "Silent Cal" Arrives

The Renaissance Mayflower Hotel was home to the first Inaugural Ball, which was held on March 4th, 1925. President, Calvin Coolidge, did not attend his own Inaugural Ball because he was in mourning; his sixteen-year old son had recently died from blood poisoning.

Vermont-born Calvin Coolidge, who served as president form 1923 to 1929, may be best known for his silent demeanor. He once explained to Bernard Baruch why he sat silently through interviews: "Well, Baruch, many times I say only 'yes' or 'no' to people. Even that is too much. It winds them up for twenty minutes more."

In 1937, the date of the Inauguration and of the Inaugural Ball was changed from march to January 20th. After this date change, the Hotel started having very strange occurrences the night of the ball. The lights dim and flicker around 10:00, the time Coolidge's pending arrival would have been announced. An elevator that would have transported him to the ball will not move until 10:15—electricians have checked but can not find any electrical problems.

Perhaps President Coolidge is finally enjoying his Inaugural Ball.

THE RENAISSANCE MAYFLOWER HOTEL
1127 CONNECTICUT AVENUE

## The Octagon House

This house was built in 1799 by Colonel John Tahoe and was used by President Madison as his temporary home after the British burned down the White House during the war of 1812. There is no record of James and Dolley Madison encountering the ghost of John Tahoe's daughter, who died in the house shortly before the war broke out.

The unusual-looking Octagon House was designed by Dr. William Thornton, who was also the architect of the United States Capitol. The Octagon had a beautiful marble entrance with a dramatic spiral staircase leading up to the upper two floors.

The Octagon was witness to the tragic death of Tahoe's pregnant older daughter, who either jumped or accidentally fell from the top banister railing into the marble foyer after her father banished her British soldier lover, refusing them permission to marry. She and her father argued and she ran up the stairs only to fall to her death. Her ghost still roams the house.

After the Madisons moved out, and Tahoe moved back in, he had an argument with another daughter. This daughter had married against his wishes. She came for a visit, hoping to reconcile with her father, begging him to accept her husband. She was following him down the stairs and tripped and fell, breaking her neck. The staircase had claimed two lives.

The two sisters now haunt the staircase where they fell to their deaths. There are cold spots felt on the staircase, strange noises are heard, candles are seen floating, apparitions appear, looking frail and faint. The father, too, has been seen pacing in the marble foyer. There are other ghosts present: some ghosts of slaves have also been seen. And, at times—even Dolley Madison.

John Tahoe died not long after the death of his second daughter.

Today, the American Architectural Foundation owns the Octagon House, and it is a museum devoted to architecture and design. The AIA moved its headquarters to a newer building directly behind it.

OCTAGON HOUSE
AMERICAN MUSEUM OF ARCHITECTURE
1799 NEW YORK AVENUE NW

## The Fugitive: Booth Continues to Haunt the Ford's Theater Murder Scene, Or does He?

Except for the assassination and storm of controversy surrounding the death of John F. Kennedy, there is arguably no chain of historic events so shrouded in mystique and myth than that associated with John Wilkes Booth following the shooting of Abe Lincoln at Ford's Theater in Washington D.C. Today, that mystery continues to surface as Booth's ghost continues to haunt and taunt visitors to the renovated museum and playhouse.

Or does it?

Ford's Theater is perhaps the most famous theater in the nation. On April 14, 1865, during the performance of Our American Cousin, John Wilkes Booth entered Box Seven and assassinated President Abraham Lincoln. After firing the fatal shot to Lincoln's head, Booth jumped from the president's box to the stage, breaking his leg in the fall. He managed to escape the theater and days later, was hiding in a barn on Richard Garret's farm near Bowling Green, Virginia when soldiers surrounded him. They set the barn on fire, and Booth is thought to have died either in the blaze or the accompanying gunfire.

But, the mystery remains.

Though actors, audiences and the staff of the theater and the museum have reported seeing Booth's ghost, others argue that because of the damage to the farm where he escaped, Booth's body was never positively identified. Conspiracy theorists believe that Booth may have actually somehow escaped the carnage. But, that still doesn't explain the sightings of him at Ford's.

In addition, actors often feel an icy presence, become ill or forget their lines when standing near the spot at the left-center stage where Booth landed.

Adding to the deep mystery surrounding Booth are scores of strange facts and happenings:

Booth's alcoholic father claimed to have had "ghostly experiences."

The ghost of Mary Surratt, said to have been one of Booth's co-conspirators in the assassination plot, and the first woman ever executed for murder in the United States, haunts the Surratt House and Tavern near Washington.

The Sergeant who claimed to have shot and killed Booth was described as being a crazy man "who talked directly to God."

Many of the main characters involved in the Booth story reportedly died strange and mysterious deaths.

Lincoln's ghost is not seen at Ford's Theater, but he has been spotted across the street at Petersen House, where he was carried when mortally wounded and subsequently died.

Ford's Theater reopened in 1968, after being closed for 103 years. It is now owned and operated by the National Park Service as a living tribute to President Lincoln and the performing arts.

FORD'S THEATER
511 10th STREET, NW

## First Lady of the Hauntings

It's probably the best-known house in America. But it's unsure if every American knows that the historic house at 1600 Pennsylvania Avenue in Washington, D.C., the White House, is filled with historic ghostly figures. Several rooms of the Executive Mansion, which was built to serve as the residence of the President of the United States, are haunted.

Many of the White House ghosts are those of U.S. presidents. Abe Lincoln is one of the ghosts believed to be seen wandering around the house The ghost of William Henry Harrison is frequently heard in the attic. Andrew Jackson revisits his bedroom in what is now called the Queen's Bedroom; definite cold spots are felt and his laughter has been heard there. Thomas Jefferson has been heard practicing piano. And there are more.

She was a First Lady. And she may be the first lady of hauntings, too. Abigail Adams, wife of President John Adams, is the first known spirit to haunt the White House. From 1797 to 1801 she was the First Lady of the White House. And, after her death, she became the first spirit to be recorded as being seen at the White House.

During her time there, Abigail would hang her wash to dry in the East Room; she was drawn to the room for its warmth and bright sunlight. These days, her ghostly spirit has been seen many times and by many people hanging up her laundry in the East Room. Or, on her way there, carrying what appears to be stacks of cloths on her outstretched arms. The room sometimes smells of soapy water and damp clothes.

Abigail was the second daughter of four children born to the Rev. William Smith and Elizabeth Quincy in Weymouth, Massachusetts. Abigail was thought to be too sickly to go to school, so she learned to read by having her older relatives teach her. Fortunately, her family had good libraries, so she read the Bible and the works of Milton, Locke, Shakespeare, and others.

Abigail married John Adams in October 1764. John was an attorney who then became active in the new Continental Congress, and who was thus away for long periods of time in Boston and Philadelphia. When he was stationed in Boston, she and the children moved to Boston.

The Adams children included: Abigail "Nabby," John Quincy, Susanna (died at 14 months), Charles, Thomas Boylston, and one stillborn daughter. Their first home was in Braintree (now Quincy), Massachusetts, where they had a farm. While John was away for business or government, she managed the home and farm with the help of servants.

Some say that her happiest times were in the newly built White House, and that is why she still continues her washing chores in the East Room.

## Dolley Madison – Her Spirits Roams the City

One of the most popular White House ghosts is Dolley Madison. The ghost of the former First Lady hovers over and protects a flower garden she planted there decades ago. It is said that when Mrs. Woodrow Wilson wanted to move the garden and have parts of it destroyed, Dolley's figure appeared in front of the workers, scaring them and anyone else trying to mess with her flowers. To this day, the Rose Garden remain very much as she left it

Though the White House gardens, and particularly her beloved Rose Garden, are her regular haunts, Dolley has been known to venture away from the gardens and visit some of the other favorite spots she enjoyed while living.

The ghost of Dolley Madison can still be seen from time to time sitting in a rocking chair on the front porch of a house she occupied in Lafayette Park later in life. She also makes appearances at the Octagon House and Halcyon House, among the most haunted houses in Washington.

## Security Check: Abe Lincoln Continues to Keep Watch on America

During times of turmoil in the United States, Abraham Lincoln is said to send his inspiration and spirit back to the White House to watch over his beloved country.

It's said that Lincoln strides up and down the second floor hallway, raps at doors, and is often seen standing by the window with his hands clasped behind his back. There are numerous accounts from maids and butlers throughout the history of the White House swearing they have seen Lincoln's ghost.

On a state visit, Queen Wilhelmina of the Netherlands stayed in the Rose Room and reported hearing footsteps and a knock on her door. She opened it to find Abraham Lincoln, in a frock, topcoat, and a top hat, standing before her. She fainted.

One of the first people to have seen Lincoln in the White House was Grace Coolidge, the wife of President Calvin Coolidge—she saw Lincoln's silhouette standing at one of the windows in the Oval Office, looking out at the Potomac. Others have reported seeing him in the same pose.

Presidents Theodore Roosevelt, Herbert Hoover, and Harry S Truman all heard unexplained knocks on their bedroom door, which they attributed to Lincoln. President Truman's daughter, Margaret, claimed to have seen Lincoln's ghost. A bodyguard to President Harrison was kept awake many nights trying to protect the president from mysterious footsteps he heard in the hall. Lincoln has been sighted most often in the room now known as the Lincoln Bedroom.

One staff member claimed to have seen Lincoln sitting on his bed pulling on his boots; other staff members will not go into the Lincoln Bedroom or near that part of the White House because they feel it is too spooky. Ronald Reagan's daughter Maureen said she saw apparitions in the Lincoln Bedroom; her father's dog would bark at the door to the room but would not go in. Many overnight guests have reported hearing his phantom footsteps in the hall outside the Lincoln Bedroom

Eleanor Roosevelt claimed that she often sensed Lincoln's presence while she was working at her desk but she never saw him. She said that she found his presence reassuring.

Rosalyn Carter would not comment about the Lincoln ghost, but when Jackie Kennedy was asked by reporters, she said she felt his presence and "took great comfort in it."

Mary Todd Lincoln had a great interest in the Spiritualist movement of the mid-nineteenth century, and she became friendly with mediums, especially the Lauries of Georgetown. During the Lincoln years there were many séances in the White House, although Lincoln was not a believer the way his wife was. She wanted desperately to connect to her deceased sons Willie and Eddie; she believed she had done so, as well as speaking to the ghost of President John Tyler.

THE WHITE HOUSE
1600 PENNSYLVANIA AVENUE, NW

## Bladensburg Dueling Grounds

Maryland's Bladensburg Dueling Grounds, just across the river from Washington, D.C., was the place that became known for many as an end to a dispute, a place to uphold a code of honor, often for an insignificant reason or principle. Some of those who lost their lives here still roam the grounds, perhaps not believing they died here for such an unimportant cause. If you go there and take photos, you will likely capture orbs, streaks of light, and shadowy figures

Daniel Key, another son of Francis Scott Key, was killed here over an argument with a friend about steamboat speeds when he was only twenty years old.

Colonel John McCarty shot his cousin, General Armistead Mason, a Senator from Virginia, over the honor of a woman they both barely knew. He later regretted the duel and the reasons for it; nowadays, his ghost, in full dress uniform, wanders the grounds.

Another sad duel that led to death here was that of Commodore Stephen Decatur, a much loved husband and Naval Hero, and Commodore James Barron. The two men hated each other, Barron never forgiving Decatur for his part in Barron's court martial for cowardice. Barron had left the United States, but challenged Decatur to a duel upon his return.

The years passed, but Barron returned and called for the duel. Stephen Decatur took a bullet below his right ribs, James Barron a leg wound. Decatur's men took him to his Lafayette Square home and his wife, Susan. He died a few hours later.

Stephen Decatur's ghost has been seen wandering the land formerly known as the Bladensburg Dueling grounds, but his ghost has most often seen with his wife Susan starring out of the windows of their Lafayette Square home. The upstairs window where Stephen was often seen has been covered up, but at times Susan's low crying can be heard throughout the house, which is now a museum.

DECATUR HOUSE
748 JACKSON PLACE NW at LAFAYETTE SQUARE

BLADENSBURG DUELING GROUNDS
BLADESNSBURG, MARYLAND
Northeast of D.C. near Fort Lincoln Cemetery

Washington Walks
202-484-1565
washingtonwalks.org

# The Southeast

Cemeteries, Ivy Covered Mansions, A Certified Haunted Museum and a visit from a Pirate Ghost are just a few experiences you can expect from a visit to the haunted cities of the South.

Encounter Charleston's Pirate Ghost, travel down Nashville's Printers Alley, where the first Southern speakeasy customers were nothing but trouble.

Take in a performance at the Memphis Orpheum Theater, a stately building where the ghost of a little girl named Mary may be sitting next to you. Stay at Louisville's Brown Hotel, where the late proprietor still keeps an eye on things.

In Atlanta, at the Joel Chandler Harris Home, "Wren's Nest," the ghost of the creator of Uncle Remus may pay you a visit. A voodoo ghost haunts a cemetery in New Orleans.

The Spanish Military Hospital Museum in St Augustine has so much poltergeist activity that photos often have more spectral orbs than real people. The Hampton-Lillibridge house is recognized as the most haunted house in Savannah.

So take a walk through tree-lined streets, have a drink at a local tavern, and let the spirits tell the tales of Southern hospitality.

# Atlanta, Georgia

Atlanta is a relatively young city, built as a railroad hub; its wealth was its rail lines. In the years before the Civil War, beginning with the Western and Atlantic and Georgia, railroads joined at the expanding facility near the center of town. Other railroads soon followed the lead—the Atlanta and LaGrange, the Macon and Western, and the Memphis and Charleston, to name a few. When the War Between the States erupted, Atlanta's regional importance and transportation network made the city a target for the generals of the North.

General William Tecumseh Sherman marched on Atlanta in July 1864. The city fought back but, after many bloody battles besieged the weakened city, the city of Atlanta was surrendered on September 2, 1864. Sherman had given orders for the city of Atlanta to be evacuated and burned. A great fire ravished the city; retreating Confederate troops burned eighty boxcars of explosives causing an enormous explosion, and advancing Union soldiers destroyed the rest. Atlanta was in flames. Remember the scene in the movie *Gone with the Wind*.

When the smoke cleared, Atlanta was a ghost town, with only about four hundred buildings still standing—the rest of the city was rubble and ashes.

Atlanta is a city that, because of its history—the battles, the great fire, yellow fever and other diseases, make it ripe for ghosts.

Many hauntings occur for reasons such as lack of proper burial, desecration of graves, sudden violent deaths due to war, fire, murder, and accidents. The spirit may be caught by death unexpectedly.

## Civil War Soldiers Still Fighting

Kennesaw Mountain Battlefield is a 2,888 acre National Battlefield that preserves a Civil War battleground of the Atlanta Campaign. A battle was fought here from June 18, 1864 until July 2, 1864. General Sherman's Union army consisted of 100,000 men, 254 guns, and 35,000 horses. The Confederates, then led by General Johnston, had 60,000 men and 187 guns. Over 67,000 soldiers were killed, wounded, and captured during the Atlanta Campaign. Three battlefield areas are in Kennesaw.

Visitors have reported hearing what sounds like cannon fire, soldiers appearing in uniform, apparitions marching into battle. The morning fog carries the smell of gunpowder. Also detected in the trenches that are still visible here is the smell of cigar smoke. Some park visitors have heard whispering voices, and the sounds of marching soldiers entering battle.

KENNESAW MOUNTAIN NATIONAL BATTLEFIELD PARK
OLD HIGHWAY 41 NW
KENNESAW, GEORGIA

## Cemetery Roll Call

Many of Atlanta's founders and famous citizens are buried in Atlanta's oldest public cemetery under the magnolia trees and grand oaks. Margaret Mitchell, the author of *Gone with the Wind*, is buried here. After the Civil War, many remains were moved to Oakland Cemetery, especially the makeshift graves of Civil War soldiers who had been buried in shallow pits. A large granite memorial is the marker for the many Confederate dead. The memorial was copied from the Lion of Lucerne and it is a massive statue of a wounded lion lying on a furled confederate flag.

It is near here where visitors say that, on quiet early mornings, they have heard a muffled roll call—names being called from an unearthly source.

OAKLAND CEMETERY
DOWNTOWN ATLANTA
Open 7 days a week, tours available

## Joel Chandler Harris Is Home

This is a popular site and the former home of Joel Chandler Harris, a prominent journalist and editor of the *Atlanta Constitution*. He is best known to us as the author of the popular Uncle Remus Tales. He moved to this house in 1881, shortly after his first Uncle Remus story was published. He lived in the house until his death in 1908. The house is known as the Wren's Nest and is a National Historic Landmark. It's the oldest house museum in Atlanta. The house was called Wren's Nest after three of Harris's children found a wren had built a nest in their mailbox. They built a new mailbox so the wren could stay in the old one.

Later in his life, he built homes for three of his children on the property; two homes here are still private residences.

Walt Disney filmed *Song of the South* here in 1948, enclosing part of the porch for a cabin interior. They also moved a one room log cabin to the backyard.

Harris is said to still reside here, occupying his old study and the front porch. He was known to have been an avid gardener, and his apparition can be seen walking among his many fruit trees. He seems friendly, but just not ready to depart from the house and land that he so loved.

WREN'S NEST
1050 RALPH DAVID ABERNATHY BLVD
SW ATLANTA, OFF I-20 (exit 19)
wrensnest@mindspring.com

Atlanta has other haunted sights, including Six Flags Over Georgia, The Shakespeare Theatrical Tavern, and Metropolitan Avenue/University Park Bridge.

At this time, Atlanta does not have a Ghost Tour,
but there is a good history tour operated by
Underground Atlanta:
Guided History Tour
Underground Atlanta
404-523-2311 ext. 7025
www.underground-atlanta.com

# Charleston, South Carolina

Charleston, South Carolina is well-known as one of our nation's oldest, and most haunted, cities. The seaport was settled in 1670 by English colonists. This very Southern city has always been subject to extreme weather—hot humid temperatures, tropical storms, and fierce hurricanes. Over the years, Charleston, as an older coastal city, has experienced colonial times, slavery, piracy, blockades, the Revolutionary War, the Civil War, and everything else.

Charleston is also steeped in Gullah legend, believing that souls get trapped between this world and the afterlife. These spirits haunt the buildings, inns, graveyards, stately homes, and the harbor of Charleston.

There are many tours of Charleston. One firm offering tours is the Charleston Sandlapper Water Tours, including a "Haunted Harbor Ghost Tour." Ed Macy, a guide for the tours, told us of these ghost tales. They are contained in the books, *Haunted Charleston* and *Haunted Harbor* by Geordie Buxton and Ed Macy.

## Miss Mary watches out for the children

The house at 18 Montague Street, in Charleston's oldest neighborhood, Harleston Village, has existed in many forms over the last two centuries. It was once a luxurious urban villa, believed to have been visited by President George Washington. More recently, it has served as an apartment building housing College of Charleston students. Some of these transient residents have provided a description of the protective ghost in this once elegant home.

The deadly hurricane of 1813 wreaked fatal havoc on much of Charleston, including the house and family at 18 Montague Street. It came on a muggy August night. As the winds progressively rose, the sounds became howls, punctuated by crashing trees. From inside the house, the Walters family and servant slaves heard the intense crashing noises. The father ordered his family and slaves to move to the lowest level of the house, where the kitchen and servant quarters were.

Miss Mary, a faithful slave, was the family housekeeper and nanny. The three daughters in the family regarded her as a mountain of protection. Miss Mary did her best to calm the girls. In her sixty-six years, she had never heard the rain and the wind so angry. She was frightened herself, but knew she must never let the little ones see her fear.

Then, the entire kitchen quarter became a blur of noise and movement. The chimney began to crumble; sections of brick fell from above. Miss Mary gathered the children and fell on top of them. She absorbed most of the falling bricks, arms outstretched, shielding them. It was over within a matter of minutes. When the father rolled Mary off of the girls, they saw her face. It was serene and lifeless. She had given her life to save the children.

In 1988, a College of Charleston junior lived in a one-room studio apartment on the top floor of 18 Montague Street. On an early Friday evening, she was preparing to meet some friends for dinner. She was brushing her hair in front of a large vanity mirror when she saw, standing behind her, a very obvious and discernible form. It was an African American woman with a stoical, almost stern face. The woman wore a white bandana on her head and a loose, formless dress of the same color. She looked directly into the reflected face of the student, nodded, turned, and disappeared into the wall of the apartment.

Over the years, there have been incidents like this in different parts of 18 Montague Street. Most have been in the same top floor apartment. According to the current owner of the property, that room was once a small ballroom used on formal occasions. Almost certainly, Mary would have spent much time in that room, either tending to the guests, or quietly watching the three small children perform. Now, Miss Mary still watches out, making sure everything is all right.

PRIVATE RESIDENCE
18 MONTAGUE STREET

## The Pirate Ghost

Stolen jewelry, visions of a man in a white silhouette, and cries for water have marked the haunting at 37 Meeting Street of a pirate ghost. The lingering spirit has appeared as a blurred image of a man with his arms folded across his chest. He has been heard crying out in a desperate call for water, as if marooned.

Stories of buried treasure have also surrounded the prominent Meeting Street home since the eighteenth century. Like most of Charleston's pirate-treasure stories, the bounty has never been found. However, the pirate's spirit still lingers, stalking the plot of land where he may have been murdered by his crew—he was missing from his sloop in the harbor—after they buried their loot on the peninsula centuries ago.

During those days, pirate criminals were held for trial at what is now the Old Exchange Building and Provost Dungeon at the end of Broad Street. The dungeon, six feet below sea level, was lined with shackles for the prisoners who awaited their fate among the stench of brine while wharf rats and blue crabs drifted in freely during the nights on high tides. The building, considered one of the most historic buildings in America because of its role in the Revolutionary War, is a portal to Charles Town's past.

Just a few homes south of the spot where tormented bones finally vanished into the asphalt of modernity is the gray mansion, with its twin buttresses. The modern address is 37 Meeting Street, and it is occupied by the lingering phantom of a sea-bound cutthroat and thief. His appearance, although usually just a white, blurry silhouette with arms crossed, has given the unspoken explanation of the pirate's dress, or lack of. In a place where modesty existed until very recently, only a pirate would dare walk among the homes of wealthy society shirtless.

This ghost has been seen numerous times and caused one new owner of this home to sell it within one year's time. He sold it because he saw the ghost twenty-seven times during that single year.

One man, who grew up at 37 Meeting Street, tells of seeing the ghost as a child in the 1970s, and the encounters were intertwined with a never-substantiated story of buried treasure in the family's back yard. The ghost was blamed for missing jewelry from the boy's mother's powder room on several occasions, having been heard creaking along the stairs, and he often called out for water in the middle of the night. The boy, now a grown man, dug up the yard with his brother in hopes of finding the legendary treasure. They were not successful. But, innately they knew that the treasure, if it even existed, is what caused that marooned pirate spirit to stay alert for eternity, never to rest in peace like the dead are supposed to. Perhaps the ghost at 37 Meeting Street was double-crossed by greed and was hanged across from the waterline like dozens before him. Now, he stays around the antebellum house on Meeting Street.

PRIVATE RESIDENCE
37 MEETING STREET

Sandlapper Water Tours
843-849-8687
www.sandlappertours.com

# Louisville, Kentucky

Kentucky, the Bluegrass State, is known for its thoroughbred horses and fine bourbon whiskey—in fact, the fastest thoroughbred horses and the finest bourbon whiskey in the world. Louisville, the state's largest city, is probably most famous for hosting the Kentucky Derby, America's premier horse race. The Derby is a one-and-one-quarter mile race for three-year-old thoroughbreds and also a big party, bringing thousands of visitors to Louisville every May.

## Southern Hospitality Continues after Death

And, when the visitors come, one of the best places to stay is the Brown Hotel in Downtown Louisville. The Brown Hotel was built by local businessman J. Graham Brown, and was opened in October, 1923. Designed by Preston J. Bradshaw, the sixteen-story hotel is in the Georgian Revival style. When it opened, David Lloyd George, the former Prime Minister of Great Britain, was the first person to sign the guest register.

In 1926, hotel chef Fred K. Schmidt invented the famous "Hot Brown Sandwich," which is a broiled open-faced turkey sandwich with a special sauce.

Many celebrities have stayed here over the years. Movie matinee idol Victor Mature, a local product, even worked here briefly as an elevator operator, before going to Hollywood to star in many not-so-memorable movies, including playing a cave man in *One Million B.C.* (1940) and Samson in *Samson and Delihah* (1949).

In 1937, Louisville was hit by a great flood; the Brown Hotel stayed open, but it had three feet of water in its lobby. The bell captain even caught a two-pound fish inside the hotel. Nearly a thousand people from low-lying areas sought refuge in the Brown, and, because of the flood conditions, ended up staying for ten days. With the power out, the hotel used candles and charcoal grills to get by.

Mr. Brown, the founder, died in 1969, after living in the hotel for over forty-five years. And, the Brown Hotel was closed. The Louisville Board of Education used the hotel as an office building through the 1970s. But, in the 1980s, the hotel was renovated and reopened. In 1993, Ian Lloyd-Jones purchased the hotel.

The Brown Hotel has a statue of founder J. Graham Brown on the sidewalk outside the hotel, but J. Graham Brown, looking very much like the statue, is also seen inside the hotel. He's been seen in the lobby, and his ghostly presence has been felt in the halls, and even in the elevator. He likes to make sure everything is working the way he thinks it should, and that the Brown Hotel maintains the high standards that he strived for, and for which it became famous.

THE BROWN HOTEL
335 WEST BROADWAY,
AT FOURTH STREET

## A Lady in Blue

While we're in Downtown Louisville, we'll mention another fine hotel, now known as the Seelbach Hilton, which is just a few blocks away. Louis Seelbach opened a successful restaurant in 1874, which moved in 1880, and he and his brother built a 30-room hotel in 1886. A new, larger Seelbach Hotel opened in 1905, and it was so popular that they expanded it right away. The new expansion was opened in 1907, complete with a Billiards Hall, which appeared in the movie, *The Hustler,* starring Paul Newman and Jackie Gleason.

This larger, modern Seelbach Hotel, which was a setting in F. Scott Fitzgerald's *The Great Gatsby*, was a favorite stop, not only for Fitzgerald, but for many prominent celebrities. One of the regular hotel guests was Cincinnati gangster George Remus, who became a model for Fitzgerald's title character.

In addition, none other than the legendary Al Capone used to visit the Seelbach to play blackjack and poker, and check on his various business interests, including his bootlegging operations. Capone played cards in an alcove of what is now the Oakroom Restaurant; he appreciated the fact that the room had two secret passageways that could be his escape routes, should the need arise.

But, the Seelbach Hotel is also haunted, by the ghost of a young bride dressed in a blue dress. In 1936, when her groom was killed in an accident on his way to the wedding reception, she took her own life by throwing herself down the elevator shaft. Nowadays, her ghost, wearing her blue dress, has been spotted in the hotel in the middle of the night. Guests have also reported smelling her perfume in the halls.

THE SEELBACH HILTON HOTEL
500 FOURTH STREET,
AT WALNUT STREET, NOW MUHAMMAD ALI BOULEVARD

Louisville has
The Louisville Ghost Hunters Society
Keith Age, President
www.louisvilleghs.com
502-245-0643

# Memphis, Tennessee

Hernando de Soto explored the region near current-day Memphis in the sixteenth century. By the end of the seventeenth century, the French had built Fort Prudhomme in the area. One of the top tourist attractions in Memphis is Graceland, Elvis Presley's home. And, of course, the Sun Studios, where Elvis first recorded.

## A Tragedy By Any Other Name

Memphis is a city known, among other things, for its role in the history of music. The Blues are still played along the mighty Mississippi River and the spirits still love to roam the historical district of Downtown Memphis. If visiting this fascinating river city, and ghosts are on your agenda, then take a tour of the Woodruff-Fontaine house on Adams Avenue.

Amos Woodruff built this historical house in 1870, where his family lived until 1883, when the house was sold to wealthy cotton merchant Noland Fontaine. The Fontaine family lived there until 1929, but after that time, the house had various owners and fell into disrepair.

The house was turned into a Historical Mansion Museum in 1960. That is when the stories of the ghost of Mollie Woodruff and "The Rose Room" on the second floor began to circulate around Memphis. It seems that when Mollie Woodruff lived in the house, she was the favorite spoiled daughter of Amos Woodruff, and she had a series of very unfortunate events, all taking place in her bedroom, now known as "The Rose Room." After she was married and had her first child, the child caught yellow fever and died in "The Rose Room." Shortly after, her first husband developed pneumonia and died in the same room.

Mollie remarried a few years later only to have her next child die in the now dreaded "The Rose Room" bedroom. Although Mollie Woodruff Wooldridge Henning died in 1917, her spirit has remained in the Woodruff-Fontaine House.

The day the mansion was opened as a museum, an employee was in "The Rose Room" when a woman appeared and said, "My bed doesn't go there" and then seemingly vanished. That was the beginning of Mollie's appearances. Mollie likes to sit on the bed, and when she gets up, an impression is left on the bed linens. Strange noises are often heard coming from "The Rose Room."

Mollie also roams the house, and visitors and guides tell of various cold spots—masses of frigid air pockets, air so cold that you can see your breath.

Other activities in the house include voices and strange odors coming from the third floor, often smelling like cigar smoke. Certainly Mollie and her ghostly guests are wandering this Memphis Mansion.

WOODRUFF-FONTAINE HOUSE MUSEUM
680 ADAMS AVENUE

## Sorry, Seat C-5 Is Taken

Memphis's proud stately Orpheum Theater was built in 1890, burned down in 1923, and was then rebuilt. Once the theater was re-opened, a spirit of a little girl named Mary began making herself known. The stories of the sightings of Mary can be found in the archives of Memphis Magazines and in the historical accounts of the Orpheum Theater.

Mary is a spectral spirit, seen floating and heard singing around the Theater, at times even playing the organ. Anyone who has encountered Mary says she is a gentle but prankish sprit. She has never disturbed a performance but has played tricks on some of the actors and stagehands. Props will be moved, Organ playing even when it is turned off. Her favorite seat is C-5 and sometimes she can be felt sitting there.

There have been séances in the Theater trying to find out how she died and why she lingers. It was thought she died in the fire but then a parapsychology group determined she died in 1921 from some sort of fall on Beale Street right in front of the theater.

The Orpheum Theater was remodeled in 1982 and when it reopened in January 1984, it was to great fanfare and recognition of the re-birth of Downtown Memphis as an entertainment center with a great past and future.

Mary intends to continue her life at the theater, an unofficial mascot of the ghostly persuasion.

THE ORPHEUM THEATER
203 SOUTH MAIN STREET

## On the Banks of the River of the Holy Ghosts

Memphis also claims another interesting haunted place: The National Ornamental Metal Museum. The museum overlooks the Mississippi River and was once a hospital. It was the first museum to feature the artistry of metalworkers from all over the world. The artwork is from jewel adorned jewelry to decorative teapots, vases and cookware. The museum opened in 1979.

The grounds where the Museum now resides was once the land of the Chickasaw Indians, Hernando de Soto is said to have been here when he first saw the beautiful Mississippi River and claimed it to be "the River of the Holy ghosts". There was once an old military hospital on the grounds. The Museum is now located in what was the nurses' dorm, built in 1937.

Many ghostly spirits of the over 1,000 victims of the yellow fever that died here are said to roam the grounds; photos have been taken that pick up unexplainable light streams and orbs.

The blacksmiths that work at the Museum say that even though accounts from the Memphis Paranormal Web site claim the place is haunted they have yet to have anything scare them enough to keep them from enjoying the grounds when they take their breaks-day or night.

Perhaps you need to go there for a visit, not only for the Museum's treasures and the view of the mighty Mississippi River, but to see if you encounter these controversial spirits.

THE NATIONAL ORNAMENTAL METAL MUSEUM
374 METAL MUSEUM DRIVE

## The Lady of the Lake

Overton Park on Poplar Avenue in Memphis is the home of the Memphis Brooks Museum of Art, the largest art museum in Tennessee, the Memphis College of Art, and the Overton Park Municipal Golf Course. It is itself a beautiful tree-shaded city park, an oasis with hiking trails, tennis courts, playgrounds, and a picnic area.

On the south side of the shallow lake in the park, an apparition of a woman in her 30's in a long blue dress is seen floating over the water, usually during the late evening hours. Sometimes she approaches people with outstretched arms, but she quickly disappears if approached. It is thought that she is the apparition of a murder victim from the 1960s. A woman was brutally raped and stabbed to death at the area she now haunts.

OVERTON PARK
POPLAR AVENUE

# Nashville, Tennessee

Originally called Fort Nashborough, Nashville was founded in 1780. In 1843, the city was named the capital of the state of Tennessee, and during the twentieth century, it became the Country Music Capital.

## Reproductions of the Ghostly Kind

You can take a one-mile stroll and discover some interesting ghostly encounters in downtown Nashville, Tennessee. While exploring the home of country music, the honky-tonks, and the thrill of blues, Nashville's first entertainment hot spot was called Printer's Alley, home of many of Nashville's printing and publishing companies. The country music scene, starting in the 1930s, changed the fate of Nashville's Printer's Alley from one of commerce to one of creativity.

Printer's Alley was the original's Man's Club in the 1880's. Saloons, speakeasy's and gambling dens were peppered up and down Third and

Fourth Avenues, stretching from Union to Church Street. Men from all walks of life enjoyed what Printer's Alley had to offer. They shared the liquor, women, money, and trouble. Businessmen, lawyers, politicians rubbed elbows with the gamblers, printmakers, and laborers. The Police turned their back on anything illegal that was happening in the Alley.

Along with the liquor, women, and gambling came drunkenness, fighting and even murder. Ghost tour guides frequently talk about the chilly air circulating around the Alley, the spots and often the feeling of dread, as if something bad is about to happen. Many an amateur photographer has taken a photo in Printer's Alley to find, when the picture is developed, orbs, glowing spots, and shadowy images lurking in the Alley.

PRINTER'S ALLEY
Located between 3rd and 4th Avenues

## Ryman's Still Steaming

The famous Ryman Auditorium was built by Nashville riverboat Captain Thomas Green Ryman, a hard-drinking steamboat captain who was converted and decided to build a tabernacle to serve the city's evangelical revivals. It opened in 1892 as the Union Gospel Tabernacle. It was renamed after its founder several years later after his death.

The Ryman Auditorium is a National Historic Landmark with

roots in country music; it was the home of the Grand Ole Opry from 1943 to 1974, when the new Grand Ole Opry House opened up at Opryland outside of town. These days, you one can see all types of musical performances there, as well as a few ghostly residents.

The Ryman Auditorium is said to be haunted by troublemaking ghosts. The ghost of the Ryman, steamboat captain Thomas Ryman, is said to haunt the former church in his afterlife.

He is watching over the current scene, but he has also been known to turn the lights off and on, and cause some general havoc.

RYMAN AUDITORIUM
116 FIFTH AVENUE NORTH

## Politicians, Celebrities, and Ghosts

Another stop in Nashville is the haunted Hermitage Hotel, Nashville's first million dollar hotel, built in 1910. The finest building material was used: Russian walnut wood, imported stain glass for the vaulted ceiling in the lobby, and Italian marble for the floors.

The Hermitage Hotel was the place to be seen in Nashville during the 1920s and 1930s. The nation's leading politicians, actors, actresses, singers, musicians, gangsters and even presidents all gathered here. The Oak Bar had the longest running musical act—Francis Craig's Orchestra appeared from 1929 to1945 and was broadcast live on the radio. Dinah Shore was introduced here. The hotel guest list included some of the most famous people of the day—Bette Davis, Greta Garbo, Gene Autry and his horse Champion, Eleanor Roosevelt, Woodrow Wilson and even Al Capone.

Later Senator John F. Kennedy used the hotel for his 1960 presidential campaign headquarters and came back later, when he was president. Minnesota Fats played pool here regularly for eight years, with his own pool table set up above the lobby on the hotel's mezzanine.

With all this excitement, is it any wonder that employees, guests, and visitors to the hotel talk about feeling as if someone is watching—the energy level is very high and the temperature in the hotel fulgurates unnaturally so. The sound of a baby crying is also heard.

The hotel was also a center for demonstrators for both the pro- and anti-women's suffrage movements; many a demonstration took place in front of the hotel. Sometimes you can hear a faint shouting noise in front of the hotel, perhaps left over from a highly charged time in our political history.

THE HERMITAGE HOTEL
231 SIXTH AVENUE NORTH

## Can't They Get Along?

It is said that The Tennessee State Capitol Building is haunted by the building's architect, William Strickland, a respected Philadelphia architect. Completed in 1859, the building is a highly regarded Greek Revival style building. Strickland, whose career began with an apprenticeship to Benjamin Latrobe, the first architect of the U.S. Capitol, had been forced, because of financial issues back home, to look for building commissions in the South. He thought his stay would be only temporary and he would return to Philadelphia some day.

The budget for the new State Capitol was limited and Strickland was forced to work closely with the construction company and its manager, Samuel Morgan, something he hated to do. Morgan made sure that nothing got past him, and he continually irritated Strickland. They argued constantly and even occasionally had to be stopped from actually hitting each other.

Unfortunately for William Strickland, he died in Nashville before the building was completed, never getting back to his beloved Philadelphia.

To honor him, the State elected to bury him on the Capitol grounds in a special burial vault. They then decided to honor and bury Samuel Morgan the same way when he died. Strickland and Morgan are both buried on the Tennessee State Capitol grounds.

Now, these two people would continue their contentious relationship into the afterlife. State Capitol guards patrolling the grounds have heard loud arguing and shouting matches, but when they try to find real people, there is no one there. This happens near the burial site.

In addition, if people are behaving in a way that is misusing the building, they may find themselves being pushed, or they hear distant voices telling them what not to do. Doors have been known to open and close, lock and unlock, seemingly by themselves.

It appears that Strickland and Morgan may continue to fight and squabble over their disagreements but they do agree on how they want their building to be respected.

THE TENNESSEE STATE CAPITOL
CHARLOTTE AVENUE
Between Sixth and Seventh Avenues

## Sad Sisters Still Lingering

The High Five Entertainment Building, formerly the Nashville home of Capital Records, is built on the site of a turn of the twentieth century mansion built by Jacob Schnell. The mansion was huge, but despite the grandeur, the Schnell family was still snubbed by Nashville's high society.

After their father's death, his two daughters became very withdrawn; they let the house fall apart, not having the disposition or means or to keep the grand house up. They lived in the house until their deaths, very much the strange reclusive Schnell sisters. When they died, the house was demolished and Capital Records built their offices on the site.

Once the building was finished, employees began seeing the two sisters walking around the building, opening and closing doors and windows. Visitors also noticed that certain offices were very cold and equipment was turned on or tampered with, strange noises would come from rooms that were unoccupied. A psychic once investigated the building and noted a great sense of loss and sadness, as well as a male presence besides the sisters. Perhaps their father was still trying to make life right for them.

THE HIGH FIVE ENTERTAINMENT BUILDING
3322 WEST END AVENUE
Private Offices

Be assured: you may also encounter ghosts at Opryland and Music Row.

Nashville Ghost Tours
1-888-844-3999
www.nashvilleghosttours.com

# New Orleans, Louisana

"'Unique' is a word that cannot be qualified. It does not mean rare or uncommon; it means alone in the universe. By the standards of grammar and by the grace of God, New Orleans is the unique American place."

—Charles Kuralt, from *Charles Kuralt's America*

New Orleans, nicknamed "The Big Easy," is a city rich in superstition. French, Creole, African-American culture, and Catholicism mixed with Southern America created a culture of magic and spirits. As Charles Kuralt says, New Orleans is unique, and is not like anywhere else.

The historic core of New Orleans, including the Central Business District, the French Quarter, and the Garden District, was largely left intact by 2005's Hurricane Katrina; the areas most often visited by tourists were not destroyed by the storm and flooding. In any case, the ghosts are still haunting the city.

## The "Translucent Man" Haunts the Castle Inn

Andy Craig, one of the owners of the Castle Inn and the Creole Gardens Guesthouse Bed and Breakfast, shared with us his stories of the ghosts haunting the two places. He will tell you that his B&B has been featured on the Travel Channel's "Most Haunted B&B's and Guesthouses." Andy told us the stories of the ghosts that haunt the 1891 Castle Inn of New Orleans.

When they first took over the 1891 Castle Inn in 1998, they had no idea we would be sharing the mansion with spirits. When one of the staff repeatedly reported seeing a male apparition standing by the window in Room 11, they didn't quite believe it. Then, when guests reported strange occurrences taking place fairly regularly, they began to think that there might be something to it. Intrigued and bewildered, they went to the previous owners and asked if they had ever encountered anything out of the ordinary. They claimed they had not.

Guests and employees have reported strange and unexplained events: objects moving by themselves, electric lights and appliances turning on and off on their own, unexplained sounds, lots of footsteps, water faucets turning on and off in empty bathrooms, and brief glimpses of a "translucent man" standing on the front porch late at night. "The kind of stuff that makes you question precepts of reality and mortality."

What Andy thinks is that they have two ghosts, perhaps more. Dates and names are hard to determine, but based on what they could learn, both of the ghosts left this material world at least one hundred years ago.

The first ghost was a paid servant who acted as a gentleman's gentleman. He was a light-skinned black man who spoke several languages, loved the ladies, loved music, drank far too much, smoked, and was quite the prankster. Sadly, he died in an accidental fire, set either by his smoking in bed or by knocking over a heating pot. His spirit remains in our mansion because it chooses to. After all, he always believed that his rightful place was in the main mansion and not in the servant's quarters. He is the one responsible for the coughing and whistling heard in the hallways, objects moving or being hidden, and he is the "translucent man" often seen in mirrors or briefly seen out of the corner of guest's eyes. He loves to play with radios, televisions, ceiling fans, and lights. He likes to move things around—if you can't find an object in your room, look in a drawer or in a place where you would not ordinarily leave it.

Their second ghost is a little girl who drowned in a small pond on the grounds of the former plantation that existed here before the property was subdivided. She was wearing a white dress and was barefoot at the time. She wanders the neighborhood in search of her mother and is a frequent visitor to the Castle Inn. She is the one responsible for water turning on and off, women being touched on the leg (as if brushed by a cat), beds bouncing up and down (as if your kid were trying to wake you up in the morning), and the sound of little bare feet running up and down hallways.

Guests have indicated that they were not frightened by their encounters, just perplexed and bemused. Interestingly, some of the "best" encounters come from guests who did not know the Inn had ghosts, or discounted the whole thing as a marketing gimmick. The Inn has had dozens upon dozens of very vivid tales told by guests who have nothing to prove or gain by their stories.

Here are a few of the spirited encounters recorded by guests in the Castle Inn of New Orleans Guest Book, which you can also read on their web site: Large shadows moving around the room; objects being moved or hidden; the smell of smoking although the Inn is non-smoking; footsteps being heard up and down the hall in the middle of the night; beds shaking; something brushing against their legs, like a cat; mist-like shapes hovering over the beds; the feeling that they are not alone in their rooms.

"Come stay with us," says Andy Craig. "Maybe you will get lucky and have an experience. If you do, tell us or write them down in our guest book. We won't laugh (although your friends and family may think you had too good of a time in ol' Nawlins before you went to bed.)."

1891 CASTLE INN OF NEW ORLEANS
1539 4th STREET
www.castleinnofneworleans.com

## A Ghostly Breakfast Buffet

Andy Craig and his partner have also purchased another guesthouse, the Creole Gardens B&B, and it turns out that it too is a place of paranormal activity. The renovation was completed recently, but some stories came up during the renovation work. A subcontractor told them: "You have ghosts!"

On one occasion, he was standing just inside a huge room with fourteen foot ceilings and nine foot high Louisiana style, 2¼ inch thick, 400 pound doors, scoping out the best way to begin demolition of the plaster without hurting the details. The door which opens inward slammed shut behind him with such force that it shook the whole building. He pulled the door open and there was no sound or movement in the three story tall antebellum hallway—there was no one there. He was completely perplexed because there was no wind that day, all the windows were closed, and the only way to shut the door was to either have pulled the door shut or pushed it from the inside.

Another story was told by the construction person: he heard someone in the bathroom thumbing their way through the pretty tiles that he had left there a few minutes earlier, as if they were looking at the patterns. He thought it was his assistant, and he called to ask him to help with setting a door. When no one answered, but the tile clacking continued, he asked again, in a louder voice. Still no answer. Finally, he got up and marched around the corner into the bathroom, only to find no one there. The tiles, however, had been laid out on the tile counter.

There are also stories from guests when they come down for breakfast. One told us of a man who sat on the edge of her bed and spoke to her in a soft "romance" language like Portuguese or Spanish. Another tale is of a woman guest who came running out of our Bordello Room 4 at 10: 30 in the morning. She was half-dressed and visibly shaking from fright. She said she was putting on her makeup in one of the bedroom wall mirrors and was shocked to see an old black woman, dressed in a simple smock, standing in the corner of the room with her arms folded across her waist, as if waiting for orders from her mistress. When she turned to see who the woman was and how she had gotten into her room, the room was empty. She came flying out into the courtyard in a panic; it took half an hour to calm her down.

Lily, the guesthouse's manager, told of some guests seeing a woman with a pearl necklace drifting around the mansion. The housekeepers also complain that they feel as if they are being watched, and they see dark blurs scurrying by them.

CREOLE GARDENS GUESTHOUSE
1415 PRYTANIA STREET
www.creolegardens.com

## It's a Voodoo Queen and a Priest Who Haunt French Quarter Cemetery

The Old St. Louis Cemetery in the French Quarter hosts one of the most famous, or infamous New Orleans ghosts: Marie Laveau, the nineteenth-century Voodoo Queen. Marie was a free woman, not a slave, because she had a white father. She became a "Voodoo Legend" in her own lifetime. Many people, both black and white, came to her small house on St. Ann Street for her powerful cure bags of roots, herbs and charms. She was known for both good and Black (bad) Magic.

Because of the high water table, the tradition in New Orleans was to bury people in tombs and mausoleums, above ground. When Marie died, she was supposedly entombed in the Old St Louis Cemetery, the most famous of New Orleans cemeteries, also known as St Louis Cemetery No. 1. There are other theories as to where she might be buried but most Voodoo devotees and curious onlookers believe the unmarked white two- tired stone tomb is that of her and one of her daughters, Marie II. Tokens of affection and offerings such as coins, pieces of bones, herbs, and flowers are routinely left at the gravesite. These are left out of great respect for the Voodoo Queen and the belief that even in death she will bestow good luck and blessings on the living.

Many believe Marie returns once a year on St John Eve to join with her followers in worship. She has been seen in the graveyard as well as just outside the cemetery. She is recognized by her "Tignon", a knotted handkerchief that she always wore.

In the 1930s a reported incident happened in a drugstore near the cemetery. A customer not knowing anything about the famous Voodoo Queen, was talking to the druggist, when an old woman came into the drugstore with a "Tignon" and flowing white dress. The druggist took one look at her and ran into the back of the store. The customer turned to the women and she began laughing. She then spoke, asking if he knew who she was. When he replied "No," she slapped him across the face and ran out of the store, vanishing over the cemetery wall. When he came to, he was told who had just slapped him.

Others believe Marie Laveau haunts the cemetery in unrecognizable forms. They say she is a large black dog, one that is frequently spotted roaming the grounds, or that she flies over tombs in the guise of a giant black crow.

Certainly Marie's presence in the Old St. Louis Cemetery is one of the best-known tales of New Orleans, but the cemetery has many other spirits.

One such spirit is Father Pere Dagobert. In 1764, New Orleans was ceded to Spain. The French who lived in New Orleans tried in vain to reverse the decision. When attempts failed, a rebellion against Spanish rule broke out, led by six French men. The five principal leaders of the rebellion were eventually caught and killed by a Spanish firing squad. The sixth member died later of bayonet wounds. After the six men were all dead, Don Alejandro O'Reilly, an Irishman fighting for Spain and commander of the Spanish fleet, ordered that the men not be buried. He ordered that the corpses be left out in the open to rot.

Legend has it that late one night, Father Pere Dagobert, beloved priest of the New Orleans colony, was able to arrange a proper burial at the cemetery for the men. These days, visitors say they hear his voice clearly singing in the early morning; the priest is there to continue to watch over the men.

The Old St Louis Cemetery is located on the edge of the French Quarter. For many reasons it is advisable to go there during the day, and with another person or two.

OLD ST. LOUIS CEMETERY
RAMPART STREET

# Savannah, Georgia

Savannah, a city established on the Savannah River, is rich in history and is one of America's most interesting and beautiful cities. But, it is also one of our most haunted cities. This Southern city offers numerous ghost tours, far more than other cities of the same size, partially because of the deep emotional connections people here have experienced over the years. The city is the site of many battles from the Revolutionary War days to our nation's bloodiest conflict, the Civil War. There are many lost souls and spirits in Savannah.

However, Savannah's spirit world is not just about phantom soldiers and battlefield victims, but about tales of love, greed, betrayal, fevers, bad weather, fires and murder.

Many of the earliest settlers of Savannah, just inland from the sea, were traders, colonists, and slaves. Pirates and sailors also claimed the city. These disperse groups came together with wide ranging social and religious beliefs; Savannah developed its own brand of social structure, one with some occult leanings (including voodoo), and a strong belief in good and evil.

The historical district can be especially eerie, with its old live oak trees, old stately homes with Spanish moss clinging to many of the iron gates and porches.

## A Crying Child, A Stunning Statue, and A Ghostly Party

This cemetery is a must see on any tour of Savannah. If you are on your own, and are not brave enough, bring another person with you—this cemetery is definitely haunted.

The land the cemetery now sits on was once a private estate named Bonaventure. It was built by Colonel John Mulryne around 1750. The Mulryne Plantation was a Southern-style mansion, with hanging moss beautifully draping the numerous terraces, and dozens of live oak trees on the grounds.

Josiah Tattnal married Colonel Mulryne's daughter and they, too, lived at the plantation home. Tattnal and Mulryne were British loyalists and, in 1777, the estate was seized and given to patriot John Habersham. But, after the Revolutionary War, Josiah Tattnal Jr. returned from England and bought back the family estate.

One night, during the 1780's, Josiah Jr. gave a party, and, when a fire broke out, the guests were moved outside to continue the partying. This was the very last dinner party at the Bonaventure, as the estate burned to the ground.

The Mulryne and Tattnal families continued to use part of the grounds as a family cemetery. Around 1848, a third generation of Tattnals, Commander Josiah Tattnall, sold the land, but putting aside 70 acres for a private cemetery. In 1907, the city purchased the cemetery from a private firm and officially renamed it Bonaventure

Cemetery. Thus, the family cemetery became the foundation of the future Bonaventure Cemetery.

The cemetery is known for having several resident ghosts. Many a story is told of pale ghostly figures appearing, often in outdated dress. One seen most often is a ghost of a little girl, Gracie Watkins. She was a beloved daughter and died from pneumonia in 1889, at the age of six. A life-size statue of Gracie sits above her grave. John Walz sculpted a life-sized marble sculpture a year after her death, using a photograph of Gracie. The inscription by her parents is worth reading.

Gracie is heard crying at night. Some visitors, touched by her cries, leave gifts and trinkets in her statue hands. She is also seen wandering through the cemetery, hopelessly lost and sad.

Other visitors tell of hearing the sounds of a party—peoples' conversations, the clanking of dishes, glasses touching, laughter, and music playing—all near where the Mulryne-Tattnal house burned down so many years ago.

Packs of roaming wild dogs are heard, but never seen, in one section of the cemetery's grounds. The barking scares many a visitor away.

However, the cemetery is most famous as an important site in the 1994 book, *Midnight in the Garden of Good and Evil;* part of the story takes place in the cemetery.

Many of the strange visions and emotions are coming from the famous and not-so- famous who are laid to rest here. Among the famous, musician and songwriter Johnny Mercer and poet and writer Conrad Aiken, both hometown boys, are buried here. Their spirits may join the revolutionary and civil war soldiers to make their own type of ghostly magic at the Bonaventure Cemetery.

BONAVENTURE CEMETERY
330 BONAVENTURE ROAD

## The Most Haunted House in Savannah

The most haunted house in Savannah, and one of the most haunted houses in the country, is the Hampton Lillibridge House. Built in the 1790s by Rhode Islander Hampton Lillibridge, it has a New England style of architecture and does look a bit out of place in the south. The house is one of the few survivors of the 1820 Great Fire that ravished much of downtown Savannah. In its history, the house has functioned as a boarding house; with its location not far from the sea, sailors boarded here, and one distraught sailor hung himself in one of the upstairs bedrooms.

Bought in 1963, the house was moved to its present address on St. Julian Juniper Street by Jim Williams, an antique dealer who was also one of the main characters in John Berendt's book, *Midnight in the Garden of Good and Evil.*

For those who were those involved in the house's move and the restoration project, the experience came with overactive poltergeist activity. Before the renovation started, they found the skeletons of eight people, probably victims of yellow fever who were buried in a hidden crypt in the building's basement. During the restoration, workers constantly walked off the job, claiming they heard mysterious knockings, tools disappearing then re-appearing, footsteps on unoccupied floors, and a very real sense of being watched. One young worker said that he felt as if some force was pulling at him, the pulling coming from underneath the floor, trying to force him through a crack in the floor in an upstairs bedroom. In the room where the sailor hung himself, workers felt cold spots and, on one occasion, they saw a shadowy figure hanging from the ceiling.

At night, when the house was supposedly empty, neighbors would see a man peering out from the third floor window. He was dressed in old fashioned clothes, wearing a bow tie. People walking by the house said that they heard women's screams coming from the house.

Jim Williams moved into the house before it was completely renovated, and he also had strange experiences—strange noises, the sound of footsteps in empty rooms, and his bed was moved while he was in it. A ghost-hunting group informed him that at least six different spirits resided there.

Jim Williams became famous for his murder trails, and his life story was immortalized in *Midnight in the Garden of Good and Evil,* which was also made into a movie, with Kevin Spacey playing Mr. Williams.

This is a popular stop on most ghost tours, and they will certainly bring up the 1963 exorcism. An exorcism was performed on December 7, 1963 by a bishop of the Episcopal diocese of Savannah, and it supposedly worked for a year or two. However, Jim Williams said they came back, and he chose to move to the Mercer House on Monterey Square.

HAMPTON LILLIBRIDGE HOUSE
307 EAST JUNIPER STREET
WASHINGTON SQUARE
(Private Residence)

## More Rum, Please

Ghosts in Savannah are found in the cemeteries, old mansions and houses; but, they also have a great fondness for the old taverns. The Pirates' House Tavern, located on Broad Street, first opened its doors in 1753. Swatch and pirates were their first customers. The tavern was immortalized in R.L. Stevenson's classic "Treasure Island". Captain Flint, who had buried his treasure on Treasurer's Island, died in an upstairs room here. Employees have reported strange noises coming from the second floor, and The Herb House, one of the fifteen separate dining rooms, has poltergeist activity—items go missing only to reappear, people are tapped on the shoulders when no one is there.

It is said that the house was once the home of the infamous Pirate Jean Lafitte, but it is believed to be the ghost of Captain Flint that appears most often. His ghostly apparition walks the halls, whispering softly that he needs more rum. His ghostly figure is not pleasant-looking; his scarred face frightens everyone who encounters it.

When the house was being renovated some years ago, a secret underground passage was discovered. The tunnel lead out to the river docks; it was quite wide and was used for quick escapes, smuggling contraband goods, women, and slaves out to the sea. Captain Flint's ghost has been spotted in the tunnel.

A brave police officer ventured deep into the tunnel when he heard voices of men and the sounds of something large being dragged; he was stunned to see, in the distance, men pulling a body and then disappearing into the wall. The owners decided to seal both ends of the tunnel and today you can see only the sealed brick wall.

The Pirates' House Tavern has had so much abnormal activity that when a National Ghost Chasing Society group came to check out the second floor, their plan was to stay a few days, monitor the temperature, take pictures, and experience the energy in the house. The group was made up of about twelve people, but after they went upstairs to stay the night the atmosphere and temperature kept changing, they heard weird noises, and an intense feeling of panic surrounded the group. All but three decided to leave the house. The group was convinced that the Pirates' House Tavern still harbored the many spirits of past pirates, buccaneers, sailors and scoundrels.

If you decide to visit the Pirates' House Tavern, please be aware that, although there is a ghostly contingent, the restaurant's food is good.

PIRATES' HOUSE TAVERN
(Now a family owned restaurant)
20 EAST BROAD STREET
Corner of East Broad and Bay Street

## No Cameras Allowed

Savannah has many haunted Inns and B&B's. You can book a room and indulge in a ghost tour around town, although some have found the ghosts at the inns a little unsettling, and so can be walking the city's haunted streets and landmarks.

One such haunted inn is the East Bay Inn built in 1852, just a few steps from the Savannah River. The Inn has a resident ghost "Charlie," who has been seen by staff and guests, and was even captured on film.

And, the 17 Hundred 90 Inn and Tavern is host to a very active atmosphere of poltergeist activity and eerie apparitions. The ghost tours tell the story of a 17-year-old girl named "Anna," who fell in love with a sailor, got pregnant, only to realize he was going out to sea and leaving her. She watched as his ship sailed down the Savannah River. She killed herself by jumping out a window.

Now, Anna haunts her old room, and other spirits haunt the kitchen and bar area. Some guests tell of their belongings going missing, often underwear and wallets, only to be found, intact, hidden in planters or bookshelves. Visitor's camera equipment will work outside the Inn, but when it is used inside, it suddenly doesn't function. But, it will work again once they are back outside. Some guests have said that batteries seem to drain quickly in the Inn.

It has happened that guests will leave in the middle if the night after being touched and feeling overcome with uneasiness. The Inn is a favorite on many tours and the hotel is more than happy to let you share in its ghostly encounters.

17 HUNDRED 90 INN AND TAVERN
307 EAST PRESIDENT STREET

Other Haunted Inn's & B&B's:
The Gastonian
Kehoe House
Marshall House
Olde Harbour Inn
The Olde Pink House Tavern

Savannah Ghosts & Walking Tours:
There are many tours and to pick the one that suits you go to
www.savannah.worldweb.com
www.hauntingstour.com

# St. Augustine, Florida

St. Augustine Florida is called the "nation's oldest city," since it has been continuously occupied since 1565, when it was discovered by Spanish explorer Pedro Menendez de Aviles. Its unique and often turbulent history has spawned more than four hundred years' worth of shadowy figures. According to local legend, there are numerous ghosts and strange goings-on throughout the city.

Some say there are so many spirits because the town itself holds so much rich history. The town of St. Augustine was founded in 1565, some 42 years before the English colonized Jamestown and 55 years before the Pilgrims set foot on Plymouth Rock

Candace Fleming, of Ancient City Tours, has worked in the Old Spanish Hospital for sixteen years and has shared some of her ghost tour stories.

## Ghostly Shadows at America's Oldest Spanish Fort

Built in 1672-1695, the oldest European fort in the United States, the Castillo de San Marcos, allowed the Spanish to control Florida for many years. But, many a flag has flown there, including the flags of Great Britain, Spain, the Confederate States of America, and the United States—all have claimed this stone fort at some time or another. It was called Fort Marion for many years.

The stories of hauntings are very consistent, and include a ghostly guard in the tower and a cloaked figure looking out from the same tower. It is said that, at times, when one puts his ear to the walls of the fort, the wall resonates with the sounds of battle. Native Americans who had been held captive here make their ghostly shadows seen roaming the grounds in the hours after midnight.

CASTILLO DE SAN MARCOS NATIONAL MONUMENT
A1A AND WEST CASTILLO

## Lost Gold

The Huguenot Cemetery, located outside the north city gates, opened in 1821, at the time of a yellow fever epidemic. It was the first Protestant cemetery in St. Augustine. Many of the bodies buried here were victims of yellow fever, and many of them were children.

It is said that children's spirits can be felt here, even floating in the trees; when pictures are taken of the trees, they have orbs in them.

One of the ghosts haunting this cemetery is John Stickley, a prominent local lawyer and judge who died when he was in Washington. But, his family brought his body back to St. Augustine for burial. The gravedigger was tired on this particular day, and he decided to take a nap, leaving the coffin unprotected. Two ne'er-do-wells saw the coffin, opened it up, and saw that the body had gold teeth. They stole Stickley's gold teeth!

When the sleeping gravedigger woke up, he discovered the body had been violated, but he went ahead and buried Mr. Stickley. These days, the Judge has been seen wandering in the cemetery in his long black burial coat, always looking down, seemingly looking for his missing teeth.

HUGUENOT CEMETERY
OUTSIDE OLD CITY GATES
ST. AUGUSTINE

## The Ghost Bride

Tolomato Cemetery is an old Catholic cemetery. It also contains the bodies of soldiers of the Civil War. Paranormal investigators have reported a great deal of activity; glowing orbs appear in photographs taken here.

At Tolomato Cemetery, there is a Ghost Bride, a young bride who died on the day she was supposed to be married. Now, she is seen among the tombstones wearing her long white dress, and her long white hair looks like a wedding veil.

One night, two children talked their aunt, who lived next door to the cemetery, into letting them camp in the cemetery. But, in the middle of the night, they ran running back to the house—they had encountered the Ghost Bride! There have been many occasions when guides and people on tours have seen her. She has been photographed floating through the headstones. One of the guides said that the best time to catch her is at 9:20.

In the old days when someone died in St. Augustine, the body was paraded through the streets to the cemetery. One story told is that of a woman whose body was being taken to the cemetery; on route, a branch from a thorny tree brushed her cheek, and she started bleeding. The pallbearers noticed this and decided to feel for a pulse. The pulse was faint, but it was there. They were able to revive her. She lived six more years, and when she died again, her family made sure that she was buried with a string and bell attached—so if she woke up she could pull it, and a bell would ring. The officials also decided to make sure there was a person stationed in the cemetery for a time after the body was buried, so that he could hear a ringing bell. Maybe this practice is where sayings like "graveyard shift," "saved by the bell," and "dead ringer" come from.

TOLOMATO CEMETERY
CORDOVA STREET
ST. AUGUSTINE

## Heartbreak Inn

At the St. Francis Inn, a nephew of the original owners fell in love with a female slave named Lilly; when his family found out, Lily was sent away. Despondent, he hung himself in the attic. Nowadays, when you go up the stairs, you will feel hot and cold spots. Showers in the Inn have been known to turn on and off by themselves; water in the bathtubs are suddenly hot and then cold.

THE ST. FRANCIS INN
279 ST. GEORGE STREET

## Ghostly Patients

The Spanish Military Hospital Museum is a reconstruction of a military hospital that stood from 1784 to1821; the museum shows what life was like if you were a patient in 1791. The museum now also houses the Ancient City Tour group, which is the only tour group that has access to the hospital.

The Spanish Military Hospital Museum is known for poltergeist activity: a bright ribbon of light streams through rooms where there is no light source; ghostly shadows walk the area, sometimes bumping into people on the tour, often confusing the tour guest who tries to figure out if it's a trick; there have been photos taken here showing orbs.

Candace Fleming, who has been working for the tour for several years, has worked in the building on and off for sixteen years. She has often experienced cold spots and sometimes when she is working alone in her office, she hears footsteps and often her office door handle is jiggled as if someone is trying to get in. Finally, the only way to make it stop is to leave the door open.

The tour starts at the museum, and, at the hospital museum, you can tour the Surgeon's Office, the Mourning Room, the Ward, and the Apothecary. The fact that there's a Mourning Room is an indication of how iffy the medical care could be.

The Museum has been certified as haunted by the Northeast Florida Paranormal Association and has been featured on the Travel Channel, TNT's "Liars and Legends," and on local CBS, NBC, and ABC affiliates.

The hospital certainly had it share of wounded, injured, amputees and dying patients from the Seminole Wars and the Civil War. In addition, it was discovered that the hospital was built on top of a Timucuan burial site. All this may explain the numerous orbs, ectoplasms, apparitions, cold spots, temperature changes, lights, shadows, and the feeling of human emotions and pain.

THE SPANISH MILITARY HOSPITAL MUSEUM
3 AVILES STREET, SOUTH OF KING STREET
LOCATED NEAR THE SPANISH QUARTER VILLAGE IN OLD
ST. AUGUSTINE

There are many more stories of ghosts and hauntings; St Augustine has 85 historic sites and many of them come with their own ghostly visitors.

Our stories are from The Ancient City Tours, Inc., who operate the only walking tour that enters a certified haunted building.

3 Aviles Street
St. Augustine, Florida 32084
Phone- 904-827-0807
E-Mail- www.ancientcitytours.net

## Stairway to Heaven: St. Augustine Lighthouse Ghosts Enchant Visitors

Just a mere 219 steps, and visitors to the St. Augustine Lighthouse in Florida have reached the top. If they're not too pooped they're in for more than just a magnificent view when they reach the top.

This black-and-white striped beauty was completed in 1874 and is one of a half dozen lighthouses still open to the public throughout Florida. (At one point there were thirty lighthouses beaming their light into the darkness).

Like most lighthouses, it eventually deteriorated from the wear and tear of the seawater and winds. But in the 1980s the lighthouse was restored. And that's when the fun began. Three ghosts-a small girl, a presence in the basement, and an unidentified man-suddenly made their presence known.

Not much is known about who these ghosts are or where they came from, but the small girl is thought to be a child who was hit and killed nearby by a train around 1900. There is a ghostly presence felt in the basement of the light keeper's house, and there have been sightings of an unidentified man, who is said to have hanged himself at the lighthouse in early years and continues to haunt the premises.

During the construction work, when the lighthouse and the adjacent keeper's house were being restored, workers spent the nights there to protect it from vandals. Reports say they would wake up in the middle of the night to see a small girl in old-fashioned clothes watching them. She would then vanish. They would also sense someone watching them during the workday and would look up and see the apparition of the man hanging from the rafters. The spirit in the basement was never seen, but workers all reported an uneasy feeling when they were in the basement alone, especially at night. There have also been stories of footsteps on the lighthouse stairs when no one was in the building. Once, when the lighthouse museum was being rearranged, a maintenance man lifted one end of a bench to move it out of the way. Before he could walk around to lift the other side, it rose up in the air and moved itself. Today, the lighthouse and light keeper's house are open to the public for tours. Visitors to the lighthouse will hear these tales discussed openly by the museum guides.

ST. AUGUSTINE LIGHTHOUSE AND MUSEUM
81 LIGHTHOUSE AVENUE

# The Midwest

Visitors en route to Chicago most likely have a list of to-dos on their itinerary–Oprah's Harpo Studios, shopping along the Magnificent Mile, hitting the restaurant and nightclub hot spots. But, from the very first moment they land in the Windy City, a thrilling travelogue of some of the most-haunted sights in the country awaits them.

From Chicago's O'Hare International Airport to the university halls of Marquette University in Milwaukee and the University of Missouri in Kansas City, to restaurants and city buildings in St. Paul and Minneapolis, Midwestern cities have a rich haunted history.

At O'Hare, the lingering spirits of the American Airlines Flight 191 crash continue to haunt Chicago residents living in areas adjacent to the world's busiest airport.

Just an hour and a half away in Milwaukee, Marquette University has stood as a Catholic institution in the Midwest since it was founded in 1881. Today there are more than 11,000 students, and also dozens of ghosts.

Cincinnati turned the Union Terminal railroad station into a great new museum, but some of the phantom train passengers are still waiting for their trains.

Many ghosts can be found dwelling at the airport, hotels, nightclubs, and various public buildings throughout Midwestern cities.

# Chicago, Illinois

Chicago is the "Windy City," located on Lake Michigan, and for many years a major transportation hub for the United States—a city that has endured political strife, gangsters, corruption, fire and naval disasters, but has thrived and become one of the most exciting cities in America. Certainly, the amount of paranormal activity experienced by its residents adds to the excitement.

## "Lights, Cameras, Action . . . Ghosts Continue to Take Center Stage at Chicago's Ford Center For The Performing Arts"

When it comes to Chicago history, most natives and historians alike will point to Mrs. O'Leary, her cow and The Great Chicago Fire of 1871 as the city's greatest tragedy. But, on a windy December day in 1903, the fire that ripped through the Iroquois Theater in the city's downtown claimed 602 lives of men, women and children, more than double that of the great fire.

The Iroquois fire was the deadliest blaze in Chicago history, and second deadliest in the United States. In the United States, the disaster was unmatched even by the Great Chicago Fire or the 1942 Coconut Grove night club blaze in Boston, which claimed 490 lives.

The fire left behind a gruesome tale and a ghostly one.

Legend has it that the location is inhabited by the victims' spirits. Inside, disembodied footsteps can be heard, and lights turn off and on during productions. In the alley, people have reported seeing a woman dressed in white meandering between the buildings. And some have felt the touch of a hand while no one is around.

Built on the location now occupied by the Ford Center for the Performing Arts (commonly known as The Oriental Theatre), at 24 W. Randolph Street, the Iroquois Theater was a ritzy performance venue designed to rival New York's Broadway theaters. A few weeks after the Iroquois opened in December 1903, Eddie Foy appeared in the musical "Mr. Blue Beard Jr." The place was packed with about 800 people and was described as a magnificent palace of marble and mahogany, a "virtual temple of beauty."

The grueling tale of the fire and how it unfolded explains a lot about why spirits continue to haunt. Ironically, when the Iroquois Theatre opened its doors on November 22, 1903, theater owners advertised their place as the only "absolute fireproof" theatre to be built to date. But just 38 days after it's opening, the Iroquois Theatre burned to the ground during a matinee performance when the drapery hiding the stage caught fire from a footlight.

Soon, the set was ablaze and panic ensued. When patrons rushed to the fire exits, they found the doors chained off. The Iroquois' owners had paid off the fire department to ignore fire code violations so that they could keep people from sneaking into shows through the fire exits. As a result, more than 600 people died from the inferno;

the floor was seven feet deep with bodies. Those who sat in the balcony tried to go down the fire escape, but when the door was opened, the people found no fire escape—just a five-story drop into the alley behind the theater. As the crowd pushed out the door, 150 people jumped or fell to their deaths.

The screams of the children for their mothers and mothers for their children are the ghosts that continue to haunt the area to this day.

The Iroquois, which sustained only light interior damage, was repaired and reopened less than a year later as the Colonial Theater. In 1926, it was torn down to make way for the Oriental Theatre, which today is part of the Ford Center for Performing Arts.

THE FORD CENTER FOR THE PERFORIMNG ARTS
24 WEST RANDOLPH STREET

## Hauntings Crank Up the Partying at Chicago's Late-Night Hot Spot

Most Chicagoans have heard the ghost stories about the popular late-night hot spot Excalibur.

The gothic building at 632 N. Dearborn St. is a popular tourist spot, located just west of Michigan Avenue. The building Excalibur occupies was built in 1892 and housed the Chicago Historical Society collections from 1892 until 1931 when the Society moved to their current Lincoln Park location. A wide variety of tenants used the building in the intervening years until it became a nightclub in 1985 with the opening of the Limelight, which later became Excalibur.

Rumors that the building is haunted began circulating shortly after the Limelight opened. Objects would move on their own. Glasses would fall and shatter for no apparent reason. Several Limelight employees reported hearing their names being called by voices strongly resembling people they knew, though that person was not there.

When Excalibur took over the space in 1989, the strange occurrences continued. Visitors experience roaming cold spots, and a manager arrived one morning to find glasses and liquor bottles smashed—but, the building's motion detectors had not gone off.

Chicago ghost tour guides and storytellers leverage the popular Excalibur's ghostly notoriety by staging shows – especially around Halloween, revolving around ghost tales and slight-of-hand illusions, offering Chicagoans the chance to kick off the spooky Halloween with a little frightening folklore.

Many of the victims of both the 1871 Great Chicago Fire and a 1915 shipwreck in Lake Michigan were brought here. Still today, many employees and patrons of this club now see apparitions and other strange happenings in the lower level of the building, which is now a restaurant and arcade.

One of the Excalibur ghosts is said to be a guy named John Lalime, who, for many years, lived more or less peacefully on a section of land on the banks of the nearby Chicago River. Near the site of the Ft. Dearborn Massacre of 1812, Lalime got into a land dispute and was murdered. Today, his ghost is said to haunt Excalibur's Dome Room.

There's a little girl who has been spotted wandering around and laughing at all hours of the day. There are mysterious candles that suddenly appear lit on a ledge some 75-feet above the floor in the Dome Room. And, in the wee morning hours, way after the staff has cleaned the place up, unexplained beer bottles suddenly appear opened and on tables along with the sounds of non-existent patrons talking away.

Other ghosts are said to be a group of women who sought refuge in the building during the Great Chicago Fire, only to burn alive. Bodies from The Eastland ship disaster of 1915 were piled in the building, which was one of many Chicago locations, another being Oprah's Harpo Studios, which operated as a temporary morgue.

EXCALIBUR
632 NORTH DEARBORN STREET

## Chicago's Randolph Street: A Journey Into The City's Violent Past

Chicago has long been touted as one of the most haunted cities in America. Some ghost hunters and researchers believe that all the paranormal activity in this city of three million is because the city sits on Lake Michigan—because ghosts like to appear near water.

There's one street - Randolph Street just west of the Loop–that has an especially dark haunted past. Today, Randolph Street is a chic corridor in the West Loop—an area that is constantly redefining and reinventing itself to adapt to the changing neighborhood and economic realities. But, formerly dubbed "Skid Row," it was also a place where two events that define the history of Chicago occurred, and continue to haunt today.

First, there's the Haymarket Riot, where a monument once stood on Randolph at Des Plaines Avenue to memorialize the eight police who were killed in a labor dispute in 1886. The City of Chicago erected a statue of a police officer in Haymarket Square on May 4, 1889. But bad luck, which some say stems from those murdered in the riot, continues to surround anything to do with the monument and its former location on Randolph Street.

The police officer who modeled for the almost 10-foot-tall statue, was thrown off the Chicago Police force, and in the 1920's, the statue itself was rammed by a street car.

After it was reconstructed, it was blown up twice in 1969 and in 1970, before it was rebuilt again and finally removed to the nearby Chicago Police Training Academy, also located in the West Loop.

Today, nothing - except a plaque honoring the Haymarket Riot - remains to mark this area today, except for the memories of the past - and the ghosts that haunt. The scene, still haunted by ghosts of the police officers, is just west of the northwest corner of Des Plaines and Randolph where the expressway begins. The plaque was installed at what was Crane's Alley from where the hay wagon and the speakers were. The bomb was thrown from this area.

Reports say that the ghosts of the Haymarket Riot infiltrate the entire Randolph Street area. Once home to Chicago's fish, meat, fruit and other food markets, and now the sight of a row of trendy eateries, but restaurant owners report that the area is still very haunted.

One of the most-haunted sights along Randolph Street is at 110 N. Carpenter Street, which is home to Harpo Studios and the Oprah

Winfrey Show. Once the home of Illinois National Guard, in 1915 it became a makeshift morgue for the 800-plus victims after the infamous Eastland Steamboat Disaster. Many of the dead and dying were taken to this spot.

The Eastland Steamboat Disaster has been dubbed Chicago's version of the Titanic, and it is one of the greatest tragedies in American maritime history. But, what many don't realize about the Eastland disaster is that the ghosts of the 800 lives who were lost continue to make their souls known, and in at least two a high profile locales throughout the city: Oprah Winfrey's studios and the Clark Street bridge, located in a hub of popular Chicago night spots.

The tragic story began in 1915 on the banks of the Chicago just steps from the Clark Street Bridge. Western Electric was treating its employees and their families to a company picnic, and nine thousand festive folks boarded four ships bound for Michigan City. About 2,500 of those folks boarded the Eastland. Even though the ship tilted perceptibly to her port side the captain made the decision to cast off. But before the Eastland could get underway, she capsized. Passengers and crew who were able jumped into the water or onto the wharf.

Despite heroic rescue efforts, 800 people died that hot July day. Once widely known as the worst tragedy in Chicago and Great Lakes naval history, the Eastland disaster has faded in memory. The Titanic was commemorated in film, and the Edmund Fitzgerald in song, but the Eastland was forgotten

But, the tragedy continues to play out in a haunting way today at Harpo Studios and at the Clark Street Bridge. Though Oprah does not grant interviews on the subject and does not discuss her own experiences, some employees' stories have leaked. Corroborated stories of light switches physically being turned back on with no one around and people being locked inside their own offices after claiming to see apparitions are just some of the things employees have told.

Security guards working the night shift reported crashing noises, the sounds of dozens of invisible footsteps marching across the lobby, phantom laughter, and the sounds of a woman sobbing. Others have encountered a ghost known as the "Gray Lady" seen floating down hallways in vintage dress. There is little doubt that the Eastland tragedy left an indelible impression upon the building.

RANDOLPH STREET
CHICAGO

## A Long-time Chicago Pub Says Cheers to the Ghosts Who Raise a Pint With Patrons

At the Red Lion Pub in Chicago's Lincoln Park, it is said that nobody drinks alone.

That's not just because having a pint at the Red Lion is a favorite pastime of Chicagoans. It's because the popular English-style pub at 2446 N. Lincoln Ave. is the home of several spirits, including a few that wander around the bar.

It's also just one of many "haunts" in the neighborhood where Al Capone once hung out. Across the street is the Biograph Theater, where the infamous "Lady in Red" fingered John Dillinger, who was subsequently gunned down by FBI agents in the alley next door.

Female patrons of the Red Lion especially must beware of the ghosts that haunt the Red Lion as they may have a hard time leaving the place. That's because a female ghost routinely locks women in the upstairs restroom. Owners say the ghost is the apparition of a woman who was killed in one of the upstairs rooms long ago, and she just doesn't want to be there alone.

The deceased father of owner Colin Cordwell also is said to haunt the Red Lion. A stained glass window above the staircase and a nearby plaque pay tribute to his father, who was buried without a headstone on his grave back in England. And a picture of the elder Cordwell hangs behind the bar.

According to Chicagoland ghost tours and guidebooks, the Red Lion is one of Chicago's most notable haunted establishments, stemming from a turbulent history dating back to the 19th Century. These days, it's also touted as having one of the city's best beer gardens.

Beer or no beer, patrons and owner Cordwell report at least several male and female ghosts who are thought to be past patrons or workers who have died in the building itself or nearby. Several séances have been held in the building to reconnect with the spirits.

Like the crowd, the ghosts represent a broad mix. There's a scruffy, swaggering cowboy in back attire, and a dark-haired bearded man and a blonde-haired man who killed each other in the bar over a gambling dispute in the early 1900s.

Sharon, a dark-haired 1920s-style woman is the infamous ghost who likes to trap patrons in the restroom upstairs—holding the door closed for 15 to 20 minutes at a time.

Other ghosts include: a 20-year-old woman who was known for wearing too much lavender perfume, and can now be detected by that same smell; a woman that died from an epileptic seizure in the restaurant area downstairs; and a malicious former tenant known as "Dirty Dan Danforth" who is believed to be responsible for an invisible force that shoved one of the owner's family members down the stairs and sent him to the hospital.

The building housing Chicago's Red Lion was originally built in 1882. At that time, the building was on the northern outskirts of the city, surrounded by farms and countryside. The Lincoln Park and DePaul neighborhoods grew up around the building, and, at times, were considered pretty rough parts of town. Al Capone hung out in this neighborhood during Prohibition when he wasn't in his corner booth at the Green Mill.

In the 1940's, the Red Lion building housed a Wild West style saloon. Later, the building became a produce store, a laundry facility, and a novelty shop. The building was rescued from disrepair in 1984 and became the Red Lion Pub.

RED LION PUB
2446 NORTH LINCON AVENUE

## Carry On Travel Superstitions: O'Hare International Airport Chicago

Flying into Chicago's busy O'Hare International Airport is getting even stranger. That's because in recent years, air traffic controllers are struggling to cope with "ghost planes" that keep appearing on their radarscopes.

What's more, the lingering spirits of American Airlines Flight

191–the worst airline disaster in the United States prior to September 11, 2001–continue to haunt Chicago residents living in subdivisions and trailer parks adjacent to the world's busiest airport. On May 25, 1979, American Airlines Flight 191 literally fell from the sky, killing all of the 271 passengers and crew members on board. The flight was meant to be a non-stop journey from Chicago to Los Angeles.

In the more than 25 years since the crash of Flight 191, many Chicago residents living next to the field where the plane crashed, have reported disembodied voices, orbs floating and strange white lights emanating from the crash site. They say dogs bark endlessly at the field where the plane crashed. Strange figures rap at their doors looking for lost luggage or saying they had to make a connection. Then, these mysterious visitors suddenly just vanish into the darkness.

Inside Terminal Two, air travelers say they have seen a man dressed in '70s-era clothing using a pay phone near the gate from which the plane took off in the American Airlines terminal.

There are lots of urban legends about this crash - including the fact that author Judith Wax, who perished in the crash with her husband Sheldon Wax, ironically, or not, discussed her fear of flying in her 1979-published book *Starting In The Middle* on page 191.

Many of the crash victims were in the publishing industry, enroute to the American Booksellers convention, which was being held in Los Angeles. Itzhak Bentov, the celebrated biomedical inventor (the cardiac catheter) and New Age author (*Stalking the Wild Pendulum* and *A Cosmic Book*) and kundalini-researcher was among the crash victims.

A number of spooky circumstances surrounded Flight 191.

Actress Lindsay Wagner, TV's "Bionic Woman," was scheduled to fly on the ill-fated plane, but she felt uneasy about it just prior to boarding. So Wagner—who believes in premonitions—decided to skip the flight, a decision that saved her life.

Beyond the horrific crash, which still continues to haunt Chicagoans and international travelers, the "ghost plane" sightings also make O'Hare a scary place. According to reports, the frightening increase in images of "ghost planes" that have been spotted in the Lake Michigan Triangle (airspace around O'Hare) in recent years, is not related to the Flight 191 air crash, but is causing its own ghostly havoc. The Triangle is an area of Lake Michigan, which runs from Ludington, Michigan south to Benton Harbor, Mich., then across the lake to Manitowoc, Wisconsin and then back to Ludington.

There, at least a dozen "ghost planes," or false radar images, have popped up on the screens of O'Hare's air traffic controllers, forcing pilots to take sudden turns unnecessarily.

Ghost hunters and UFO experts attribute the "ghostly sightings" to a recent upsurge in solar activity. It is either causing the "ghost plane" echoes themselves, or opening the Triangle and allowing the O'Hare radar sets to sweep the skies of the past, and pick up ghost sightings.

O'Hare is not the only airport to have supernatural reminders. London's Heathrow Airport is said to be haunted by several spirits. An 18th century highway man who was hung is seen riding his horse around the airport, along with a man who died in a Belgian airlines crash, who is seen on the runway near where the plane crashed.

Perhaps the most bizarre travel-related apparition sightings came after the crash of Eastern Airlines flight 401 near Miami in 1972. Eastern salvaged many parts of the fallen L1011 aircraft and used them on other airplanes. Crew and passengers alike reported seeing the ghosts of Captain Bob Loft and flight engineer Dan Repo (both died of injuries in the crash) on the airplanes with the salvaged parts. A television movie, *The Ghosts of Flight 401*, was made about the paranormal reports.

Purported apparitions on the airways are nothing new, prompting travelers to wonder: should I check my travel superstitions, or carry them on? On Air France, for example, there is no Row 13. The same is true for Air Tran, KLM, and Iberia Airlines, where rows jump from 12 to 14.

O'HARE INTERNATIONAL AIRPORT
10000 WEST O'HARE, CHICAGO

# Cincinnati, Ohio

Cincinnati has been an important Ohio River port since its founding in 1790 in what was then considered the West. (It was originally named Losantville and was renamed Cincinnati in 1790.) One visitor, Henry Wadsworth Longfellow, dubbed it "The Queen City." Another visitor, Winston Churchill, said, "Cincinnati is the most spectacular of all the inland cities in the United States."

Cincinnati has many historical sites, including the National Underground Railroad Freedom Center, which honors the runaway slaves and the people who helped them escape, and the William Howard Taft birthplace, which commemorates the only man to have served as both President and Chief Justice of the United States.

## Spirited Guides At the Museums

Cincinnati also has the Cincinnati Museum Center at Union Terminal, home to the Cinergy Children's Museum, the Omnimax

Theater, the History Museum, and the Museum of Natural History & Science. It is a nationally recognized educational and research resource, and has more than one million visitors annually. Originally built in 1933 as the Union Terminal train station, the building is a national historic landmark. It was designed by Roland A. Wank as the principal architect with Paul Philippe Cret. It was renovated and reopened as the Cincinnati Museum Center in 1990.

The Cincinnati Museum Center is also haunted. A security guard named Shirley was shot and killed on the fourth floor of the building in the early 1990s, after catching thieves of computer equipment. Today, she is still making her evening rounds. In the area of the building where the train tracks were, the sounds of people weeping or cheering are heard. The Union Terminal was a major railroad terminal during World War Two, and many of the passengers were soldiers leaving or returning.

CINCINNATI MUSEUM CENTER AT UNION TERMINAL
1301 WESTERN AVENUE

Located in Eden Park, about two miles away from the Museum Center, the Cincinnati Art Museum has free admission and an impressive collection of more than 60,000 objects. *Parenting* magazine has ranked the Cincinnati Art Museum as "The Top Art Museum for Families." There are also otherworldly spirits in the Cincinnati Art Museum. Security guards have spoken about seeing a seven-foot-tall specter that rises up from the mummy sarcophagus on exhibit there. Eden Park itself is said to have a ghost—a young woman in a black dress standing near the gazebo.

CINCINNATI ART MUSEUM
953 EDEN PARK DRIVE

# Kansas City, Missouri

Kansas City played a major role in nineteenth century American history as a gateway for pioneers heading West along the Oregon, California, and Santa Fe trails. From the visit by Lewis and Clark to the many settlers, missionaries, and traders who began their long overland journeys from the this area, Kansas City has been a gateway city.

## Traveling Home to the Rich and Famous, Kansas City Hotel Hosts its Own Distinguished Ghosts

Kansas City's Hotel Savoy is more than just the oldest continuously operating hotel west of the Mississippi River. It's also one of the most haunted places in town.

Built in 1888, the hotel was a very fashionable place up until World War II. It was an elegant stopping place for prominent travelers like presidents and the famed and fortuned, featuring intricate woodwork, a ballroom, a rooftop garden and a stained glass skylight.

Home to visiting presidents who were traveling through Missouri, the guest list included: Teddy Roosevelt, William Howard Taft, Will Rogers, Sara Bernhardt, W. C. Fields, and John D. Rockefeller.

In 1903, the Savoy Grill, one of the oldest restaurants in Kansas City, was opened. One of the dining booths is known as the president's booth-Harry S. Truman, Warren G. Harding, Gerald Ford and Ronald Reagan have all dined at it. The restaurant's murals, which portray the departure of pioneers beginning the Santa Fe Trail from Westport, grace the walls of the restaurant and have been featured in a Smithsonian Institution exhibit.

After the Second World War, the hotel degenerated into a low-rent building and became very run down. For a time the hotel was a residential building—a flophouse—with apartments.

But, owner Don Lee recently renovated the hotel into a bed and breakfast. It is once again considered a must-stop for Kansas City travelers. The Savoy, which is in the National Register of Historic Places, was used to film scenes for the movies *Mr. and Mrs. Bridge* and *Cross of Fire*.

Despite the more famed travelers, some of the guests today are rather spooky. Staff members and residents have reported ghostly phenomena: footsteps in the hallways, doors opening on their own, and appliances gone haywire.

A woman who died in the bathtub in Room 505 is said to haunt the room. Her name is Betsy Ward, and it is said that she will turn the hot water in the shower on and off to scare guests.

Another ghost is said to be a man named Fred Lightner who once lived in an apartment there. A gray specter that looks like him is often standing in the hall outside his former room. The seventh floor is also said to be haunted by a ghost who likes to slam doors and turn on the steam vent heating system, which has been capped off and is no longer used. And, some say that the basement is haunted—some employees refuse to go down there

HOTEL SAVOY
219 WEST 9TH STREET

## All Roads Lead to Kansas and Its Ghosts

Go gold and blue ... and the ghosts! These are the cheers of many at The University of Missouri-Kansas City, which has its share of spooky lore and urban legends.

The university's most famous resident ghost hangs out in the playhouse. Supposedly, the woman who now haunts died in the arms of the stage manager in 1957. The female ghost is said to be angry because of her fate. University staff and students say they feel cold spots, and that the lights are turned on and off all the time. Some have seen apparitions of this woman.

She's also got a troupe of ghostly friends.

On one occasion, a police officer reported that his patrol vehicle was rear-ended by a ghostly car, as he was parked outside the building. The officer reported that he heard and felt the impact, but when he stepped from his car to investigate he found nothing. On another occasion, the same officer and his partner reported that while they were walking through the building turning out the lights, they saw a disembodied arm covered in a blue sleeve appear and turn out a light that a few minutes earlier had refused to go out.

But, the University Playhouse is not the only haunted theater in town. Across town, the Goppert Theatre at Avila College is haunted by a workman who fell from scaffolding during the building of the theater. He has been felt backstage and in the tunnel underneath the front office - apparently, he is also a theater critic—he lets it be known if he is not pleased with the theater's latest production.

THE UNIVERSITY PLAYHOUSE
THE UNIVERSITY OF MISSOURI-KANSAS CITY

# Milwaukee, Wisconsin

French traders and missionaries were in this area as early as the late seventeenth century, but the City of Milwaukee came into existence in 1846 when three neighboring rival towns joined together. Milwaukee has thrived as a Great Lake port, and thus the city grew and developed into a dynamic industrial city.

Just an hour-and-a-half north of Chicago, Milwaukee's downtown can seem deserted compared to the hustle and bustle of the Windy City. But, buzzing beneath the surface of this city and its collection of nineteenth-century rusticated stone and Romanesque revival buildings is a hive of ghostly activity.

## The Host with the Most Dotes on Guests Forever at this Downtown Milwaukee Hotel

The Pfister Hotel, designed in 1893, is one of these—a handsome, sturdy, limestone and brick structure just a few blocks from

Lake Michigan. It is considered Milwaukee's premier hotel and has had a roster of famous guests. Marlene Dietrich and many other film stars stayed there, as did every US President since William McKinley (including Bill Clinton and George Bush). The Rolling Stones stopped at the Pfister, and national baseball teams call the hotel home when they are in Milwaukee playing the Brewers.

But, what is perhaps most distinguishing is its ghost. And its ghost is especially hospitable. Founder Charles Pfister still lingers around the century-old hotel, called the "Grand Hotel of the Midwest," seemingly making sure guests still are comfortable and properly attended to. Pfister's presence is made known as a "visitor" who has been spotted surveying the lobby from the grand staircase, strolling the minstrel's gallery above the ballroom, and passing through the ninth floor storage area. He is always described in roughly the same terms: "older," "portly," "smiling," and "well-dressed." Upon seeing a portrait of Pfister, witnesses swore that it was the man they had seen.

Rumor has it that Pfister's ghost, described as "portly, older, smiling and well-dressed," also hangs out on the 9th floor. When L.A. Dodger 3rd baseman Andre Beltre stayed here while playing the Brewers, he told *Sports Illustrated* that his room was so haunted, he only got two hours of sleep over three nights. First, he heard knocking in the hallway and on his door. Then his TV kept turning off. So did his air conditioning. Finally, he started hearing pounding noises from behind his headboard.

The hotel is known for its three-story lobby, which is fabulously lush and opulent, with gilding and an ornate white marble staircase that leads to the hotel rooms. At the other end is the attractive Lobby Lounge with its massive, French hunting lodge style fireplace and overstuffed chairs and sofas. The lobby is filled with Victorian paintings from Pfister's collection (the world's largest hotel collection of Victorian art).

The Pfister hotel is located at Wisconsin Avenue and Jefferson Street. The hotel was the dream of Guido Pfister, a prominent Milwaukeean whose fortune came from a successful tanning business. Local legend has it that the ghost of Charles, the elder Pfister's son, is the one haunting the hallways.

THE PFISTER HOTEL
424 EAST WISCONSIN AVENUE

## School Spirits Haunt Marquette University

Tucked in the heart of downtown Milwaukee, Marquette University has stood as a Catholic institution throughout the Midwest since it was founded in 1881.

Today, there are more than 11,000 students. But, there are also dozens of ghosts. Some say that Marquette is especially ripe for ghostly activities, because it sits atop sacred grounds of Native American tribes who originally settled in the Milwaukee area in the mid-1600s.

One of the most famous Marquette ghosts is a young boy called "Whispering Willie." He haunts The East Hall, once home to a local YMCA. Sadly, the little boy drowned in the Y pool, and has been swimming alongside students doing laps in what is now called the

Rex Plex Pool. Willie is held responsible for a number of unexplained events in the building: doors opening or slamming shut, flickering lights, and a whispering voice that mimics what students are saying.

Johnston Hall is another popular ghost haunt and also representing a sad event in the University's history. In 1960, two Jesuits priests, according to the story, clambered out on the fifth floor balcony and hurled themselves over the side to their deaths. Students have reported seeing pale faces of these two men in fifth floor windows. Some say that, all of a sudden, the temperature in their rooms will plummet and they'll hear unexplained footsteps and voices; they report that their laptops, cameras, cell phones, and other recording equipment frequently fail to work. At one point, to chronicle the "ghostly activities," the Marquette campus newspaper staff spent the night in Johnston Hall. The photojournalists captured a "strange human figure" in a photo, and also heard voices they couldn't explain.

Also in the basement of Johnston Hall, it is reported that a Native American spirit wanders, forever tormented that Johnston Hall sits atop sacred land that was once the burial ground for the Mascoutens tribe, first encountered by Claude Allouez in 1667. The spirit makes himself known with blasts of cold air and beams of pale blue light.

Nearby Cobeen Hall features a room where students are put to test by the ghost of a student who committed suicide in the building. If he likes the students, he apparently leaves them alone. But if he dislikes things like the decorating, he makes his feelings known—he has been known to tear down posters he dislikes.

Across the street is Tower Hall, which was a hotel in the 1950s. One day a fire raged through the building, causing extensive damage and killing a young boy. Since then, a young boy has been seen peering out of windows or calling out for attention.

The Varsity Theatre down the street features a lurid tale. A projector operator once took a smoking break near a large ventilation fan in a hallway off the balcony. Somehow his clothing was caught up in the rapidly rotating fan and the young man was sliced to pieces. He hasn't been seen, but he often renders help to the current employees, turning on lights and locking doors that the workers forget to latch.

The Humphrey Hall dormitory served as the Milwaukee Children's Hospital before 1988 when it was converted to apartments and later to dorms. The upper floors were renovated, while the lobby downstairs remains virtually unchanged. The bakery in the lobby fronts the former emergency room doors. These doors and the rooms behind them remain closed to students and staff.

Students who live on the fifth floor, which used to be the intensive care ward, say they see a little girl who wanders the fifth floor who attracts much attention. She's believed to be about nine years old, and is always seen in a white hospital gown. If she suspects she's been spotted, she runs away, disappearing around corners or even through doors. At times, she has appeared at the foot of a person's bed in the middle of the night. One of the desk receptionists has reported hearing sneezing behind him late at night, yet never found anyone. And, loud screams or the crying of children has sometimes disturbed the sleep of students living there.

MARQUETTE UNIVERSITY
WISCONSIN AVENUE

# Minneapolis and St. Paul, Minnesota

Minneapolis and St. Paul are called the Twin Cities; each lies on separate sides of the Mississippi River in eastern Minnesota. But, despite the proximity, the two cities aren't all that similar–one, St. Paul, is small, even quaint, the, other, Minneapolis, is a booming modern metropolis with skyscrapers and three major sports franchises. But, the twin cities share one thing in common: ghosts. Lots of them! Ghosts seem to be everywhere.

## Do Ghosts in the Twin Cities Come in Pairs?

In St. Paul, which lies on the eastern side of the Mississippi River, ghosts abound. There's Forepaugh's haunted eatery, Grigg's Mansion, and much more. In Minneapolis, which lies on the western side of the Mississippi River, fright-filled tales abound. And, ghosts are seen all around the North Star State!

The ghosts in the twin cities are everywhere. There are the phantom soldiers of the Civil War who walk the remains of historic Fort Ripley, near Little Falls; renovations to the elegant Fitzgerald Theater in downtown St. Paul awakened the ghost of Ben, the spirit of a stagehand; owners of an old homestead in Dakota County recognize the ghost they call Pete when they hear heavy phantom footsteps and an unseen car spraying gravel on the driveway.

The tales go on an on. Even realtors in Minneapolis offer ghost-busting services to potential buyers. Other haunted buildings in the downtown of Minneapolis include the Palmer House Hotel in Sauk Center, which is haunted by the mischievous ghost of renowned Minnesota author Sinclair Lewis.

And one of the most notorious ghosts is at The Ramsey County Courthouse in St. Paul, where the last prisoner to be hanged in Minnesota is one of many spirits haunting. Ghost hunters say the ghostly activities in this building are among the most active in the state.

Many of the ghosts seem to be nocturnal, with late-night cleaning crews and security guards reporting late night sightings, including ghosts who appear to be from the 1930s and 1940s. These ghosts are dressed in vintage clothing and roam the halls, just as if they were transplanted from a busy workday during those times. Most of these office ghosts are friendly; they are often heard laughing and talking in the empty rooms. The security guards have even spotted a shoeshine man from the era who is seen still working his trade.

There is one frightening spirit–a male criminal who hung himself in the courthouse. Evidently, he likes to plan mischief, undoing the work of construction crews during renovations of the building and disconnecting pipes so water leaks all over. Ghost hunters say he is a troubled spirit who wants to get revenge on the fate that brought him there.

RAMSEY COUNTY COURTHOUSE
15 WEST KELLOGG BOULEVARD
ST. PAUL

## Death Row Spirit Continues to Haunt Minneapolis City Hall

When visitors arrive in Minneapolis, one of the first images they see is the beautiful 57-story reflective glass IDS Center skyscraper. It has been heralded as an architectural breakthrough for designers Philip Johnson, John Burgee, and Ed Baker. Not just a tall building, it's known for its "crystal court," an impressive ground floor shopping center with a canopy of glass skylights.

But, while tourists and shoppers are buzzing at the IDS Center, other visitors may get a ghostly experience if they venture over to the old Minneapolis City Hall, which runs the block between South 4th and 5th Streets. It is on the fifth floor and in the subterranean holding cells of this magnificent historical building where visitors will find ghostly goings-on. The spirits are said to be those of former criminals who were hanged in the building before capital punishment was outlawed in Minnesota.

The ghosts themselves are notorious. One is the ghost of John Moshik, who was hung in March of 1898. His trial was held in the Chapel Courtroom on the fifth floor. During the trial, John pleaded "insanity." But, he eventually was convicted of the murder of a man during a robbery of the sum of $14. He was hung for his crime, the last man to be hung in the state.

But, he doesn't want others to forget. Visitors say they hear him walking – eerie footsteps. They also explain cold drafts of wind, and unexplained shadows of a man who looks exactly like Moshik. And, although the Chapel Courtroom was remodeled, the ghost remained and continues to haunt the fifth floor.

Moshik and other ghosts seem to be especially present in the south tower of the building, which at the time was where Death Row was located. And, it is the area where John Moskik was held. After his death, inmates reported seeing him walking through and looking into their cells. But, he was not seen on the security monitors.

Today, visitors can step back in time and experience the beauty and majesty of the historic Minneapolis City Hall building and can even rent it for special events. This building, listed on the National Register of Historic Places, features Richardsonian Romanesque architecture, a 345-foot clock tower that rivals Big Ben, a six-story Rotunda adorned with 37 stained glass windows, a skylight, Italian Carrara marble, the historically renovated City Council Chambers, and more. The clock's bells weigh from 300 pound to over three tons each. The bells are electronic now, but were originally played by a pedal keyboard, which works like a labor-intensive piano.

The City Hall and Courthouse was built between 1887 and 1906 on the site of what was once the first public schoolhouse west of the Mississippi River. When completed, the City Hall and Courthouse had more than enough room for government functions. A blacksmith shop, a horse stable, a wool brokerage, and a chicken hatchery rented the building's excess space.

After 1940, office space started getting crowded and, despite major modifications, the only solution was to construct a new building. Hennepin County moved several offices across the street into the Government Center in 1975. Today, the building is occupied primarily by City departments but still houses the Hennepin County Sheriff's Office, Adult Detention Center and Conciliation and Arbitration Courtrooms.

MINNEAPOLIS CITY HALL
350 SOUTH 5TH STREET

## There's More to the Prairie Home Companion Story Than Meets the Eye

These days, Garrison Keillor, Robert Altman, Meryl Streep, Kevin Kline, Woody Harrelson, and a host of other Hollywood celebs have made the Fitzgerald Theater in St. Paul, Minnesota a star-studded place to be. They've been busy filming a move based on "A Prairie Home Companion," the radio show that makes its home here. But, there are a couple of other stars that make themselves known: Ben and Veronica, the ghosts.

Built in 1910, the Fitzgerald Theater is St. Paul's oldest surviving theater space. Originally named the Sam S. Shubert Theater, it was one of four memorial theaters erected by entertainment-industry leaders Lee and J. J. Shubert after the death of their brother Sam.

In 1933, it became a movie house screening foreign films and was thus christened the World Theater. Minnesota Public Radio purchased the theater in 1980 and restored it in 1986 for the live radio program "A Prairie Home Companion" with Garrison Keillor.

The theater was again renamed in 1994, this time for author F. Scott Fitzgerald, a native of Saint Paul. The theater has, over the years, played host to touring Broadway musicals, vaudeville shows, film festivals, and concerts of all sorts.

It was during the renovations in the 1980s that a ghost named Ben began to appear. During the renovations, the construction workers removed a false ceiling and it revealed that there was another balcony that no one had known was there. A series of strange events began when the balcony was revealed. A ghost started walking around checking on the progress of the construction, and cold spots were felt throughout the theater. The workers also found a note in the balcony written to a stagehand named Ben–the guy who is now haunting the place. Ben is thought to be a kind-spirited, fun guy; he started playing tricks with the construction workers' tools—moving them, hiding them, having them turn up again in unusual places.

These days, Ben's name even shows up on the employee work chart.

Another Fitzgerald Theater ghost, Veronica, is said to be a former actress; she is heard singing at night, and she has left lipstick kisses on the dressing room mirrors. Veronica is believed to be an actress (and singer) who died many years ago. She does make her presence known.

FITZGERALD THEATER
10 EAST EXCHANGE STREET
ST. PAUL

## Ghostly Goings-on On the Menu at St. Paul Eatery

Today, Forepaugh's Restaurant in St. Paul is one of the most popular restaurants in town. The décor is elegant Victorian, the cuisine is fine French, and it is served in one of many rooms where St. Paul's business elite likely dined and discussed their profits and losses.

And, there is one patron who refuses to leave.

Her name is Molly, and honestly, why should she leave? At one point in her life, she was the life of the household of this opulent mansion, surrounded by finery and living in the lap of luxury. That was in the days before the Victorian house on Irvine Street was turned into a popular eatery. And, that was all before she got dumped by her lover, and, of course, before she died.

Today, Molly's spirit continues to haunt. Many patrons and even the restaurant's owners say she is St. Paul's most playful ghost, and they truly enjoy her antics.

However, her history is a sad one. Her lover and employer, Joseph Forepaugh, a 19th-century dry-goods baron and the first dry-goods person in Minnesota, committed suicide, and left Molly, his upstairs maid, with few options. He also left behind a wife and two daughters, so Molly was completely out of the picture upon his death. The home, where even though she was maid, she was also girlfriend and quite pampered, was put up for sale and she ended up with nowhere to live. Depressed, Molly then hung herself from a chandelier.

These days, Molly is quite a prankster. She'll reset all the tables after the staff has the eatery cleaned up and ready to go for the next day. There are plants that appear dry, but they will "accidentally" drip on patrons dining in one of the dining rooms. Glasses have been known to fall off shelves, candles are suddenly blown out.

Many restaurant goers and workers say they've also seen Molly. One photograph taken by a customer captured her hand reaching out of a wall.

Other guests say they ask Molly to do things. Since it's well known around St. Paul that she is the ghost of Forepaugh's and that she lived on the third floor, they go up to the third floor and tell Molly to prove her existence: "If you slam that drawer we will know you are real." And, Molly will do it—the drawer slams.

It is said that Forepaugh's is supposedly haunted by two other ghosts: a boy named Chad who opens the door for people and a former grounds keeper, who usually is seen outside.

FOREPAUGH'S RESTAURANT
276 SOUTH EXCHANGE STREET
ST. PAUL

# The West

From Vegas to the hotels of Dallas and Fort Worth, ghosts haunt the cities of the West.

From a hotel in Phoenix to a house museum in Denver and to the casinos of the Las Vegas Strip, cities in the West are host to lots of paranormal activity.

In Denver, nearly 40,000 people a year visit the Molly Brown House Museum each year to learn about the lifestyle enjoyed by Victorian Denver's upper classes and to gain a glimpse into the life of Denver's "unsinkable" lady. Others come hoping to witness some of the chilling paranormal activity experienced in the house by employees, volunteers, psychics and mediums.

Find out why the runaway bride of the Dallas landmark hotel, the Hotel Adolphus, is heard sadly crying in the night. In Houston, a boy and his dog hang around his gravesite.

In Albuquerque's Old Town the City Street Café has a ghostly helper, making sure the place is neat and tidy. And, in Salt Lake City, phantom children run through an office building.

Tourists visiting the West will find a collection of ghost tales in most of the major cities throughout the West. Just a few of the stories are here.

# Albuquerque, New Mexico

Albuquerque today is a combination of high technology and an old frontier town. Founded in 1706 by colonists who had been granted land rights by Phillip of Spain, they created a new city on the banks of the Rio Grande.

## Healer Still Haunts With her Ghostly Touch

She was known as a "curandera," or healer. These days, Sara Ruiz's spirit continues to loom large at the Church Street Café nestled in the heart of Albuquerque's Old Town district.

This 18-room hacienda dates back to 1709. Originally built as a residence by the Ruiz family, it was referred to as the Case de Ruiz for over 200 years. It was built around the time of the founding of Albuquerque; it remained in the Ruiz family until the last family member, Rufina G. Ruiz, died in 1991 at the age of 91.

But, when the property was purchased, and renovations began to turn it into the Church Street Café, Sara, Rufina's mom, began to make her presence known. It appears Sara was not happy with the renovations as she once yelled at a contractor, "Get out of here, now!" During the construction work, buckets began to mysteriously get kicked around. The new owner decided to speak to the spirit, and, after that talk, Sara allowed the work to continue.

These days, employees of the café have seen Sara's spirit dressed in a long black dress; a number of customers have also felt her presence. Many believe that Sara's spirit haunts to make sure the café has the respect it deserves. Sara greets employees every morning and bids them good-bye every night.

Sara is often seen sweeping or dusting when she appears.

The house was originally built in the hacienda style, the classic Old Spanish U-shape. It remained this way with only minor changes until 1920 when a flood destroyed half of the house. The map shows the house on School Street (now Church Street) across from the San Felipe de Neri church. The back parking lot of the church was once the original Old Town Plaza and the current convent structure on the church was an old Catholic school.

CHURCH STREET CAFÉ
2111 CHURCH STREET
OLD TOWN

# Sad Legacy of Little Boy Continues to Haunt KiMo Theater

Known for its Native American pueblo motif, the KiMo Theater in Albuquerque was opened in 1927 as a moving picture palace. The creation of this beautiful, Southwestern-style theater was financed by a hardworking, wealthy entrepreneur, Oreste Bachechi, who wanted to fulfill a lifelong dream of building a grand theater, which would rival other larger-than-life movie palaces that were springing up around the United States.

During its heyday, the KiMo, which means "king of its kind," combined the best of live performances with both silent films and talking productions. Celebrities such as Sally Rand, Gloria Swanson, Tom Mix, and Ginger Rogers all performed on its grand main stage.

But tragedy, however, marred its success. On August 1, 1951, a six-year-old boy named Bobby Darnall went to the theater to see a matinee of "Abbott and Costello meet The Invisible Man." During the show, he exited the theater to get popcorn from the lobby concession stand. While he stood at the counter, a water heater exploded, injuring several, but little Bobby was killed.

Today, Bobby, a kind, shy boy is still omnipresent at the KiMo. He is one of the resident ghosts, and the most popular and well-liked of the paranormal guests. Wearing a striped shirt and blue jeans, he often is seen playing on the lobby staircase. But he is also known to play numerous impish tricks, such as tripping the actors and creating a ruckus during performances. To appease Bobby's spirit, the cast hangs doughnuts on the water pipe that runs along the back wall of the theatre behind the stage. The edibles mysteriously disappear.

A year after the KiMo Theater opened, Mr. Bachechi died suddenly, leaving the KiMo Theater to his sons, who expanded the scope of the theater by offering vaudeville and out-of-town road shows as well as continuing to show films.

Like many old grand theaters, the KiMo slipped into disrepair during the '60s and '70s and was scheduled for the wrecking ball. It got a reprieve in 1977, when the citizens of Albuquerque got together and purchased the old theater with a $324,000 bond, which started the very long process of renovation and restoration. The last restoration project was completed in 2002, when the third floor was renovated.

These days, there are many ghostly appearances at the KiMo. An apparition of a lady in a bonnet can be seen walking down the halls, going about her business. Not much is known about her.

And, Bobby still haunts the theater; he is well behaved—as long as his donut treats are hanging on the water pipe. Most sightings of Bobby, however, seem to center around the casts of the live performances that take place at the KiMo now. For a period of time, it seemed that not one performance went off without some type of disaster. Between actors locked in their dressing rooms, tripping while making their entrances, many of which were accompanied by child-like laughter, it seemed the little boy was bent on wrecking the business. His activities, however, sparked a strange tradition that lasts to this day.

On a typical night, the scenario goes like this: The theater lights dim, as the show is about to start. The crowd finds their seats and the conversation dwindles to a murmur. In the darkness, a patron spins in her seat, as though icy hands had just run up her spine. She glances about, her eyes finally settling on the balcony, where a small child, far too young to be in attendance alone, waves to her with a gleam in his eye. She doesn't know why, but the boy frightens her. A man draws her attention at center stage, which thanks the audience for coming, thanks the patrons, and, as a final note, thanks "Bobby."

KIMO THEATRE
423 CENTRAL AVENUE, NW

## Stop The Presses: Ghosts Head the Club

When it was built in 1903, the Albuquerque Press Club was a family home, designed by architect Charles Whittlesey. It was appropriately dubbed the Whittlesey House and was located on the western edge of Albuquerque, New Mexico. Over the years, the building changed hands many times, and, today it is known as the Albuquerque Press Club. It is a club for men and women engaged in the profession of journalism and related fields.

Most of the ghostly phenomena are the sounds of past patrons walking around the place; the click-click of high-heeled shoes are often heard walking across the bar and lobby areas. Strange voices are sometimes heard; at times, the piano is heard playing, but with no pianist. Cats at the club have been observed watching and hissing at an unseen presence.

The apparition of a woman in a black shawl that the staff calls "Mrs. M" has appeared to numerous people over the years. Mrs. M. is a former owner who is seen walking around the club. To understand her desire to stay, it is important to understand the kind of institution she transformed the house into. Many say she is still caring for the souls she welcomed into her home.

During the last century, the three-story framed subject, unique with its Norwegian villa low pitch roofs and exposed log-cut facades, has changed hands many times. It has been a family residence, a nightclub, a fraternity house, and, during Mrs. M's time, she once rented rooms to patients from nearby sanitariums who were convalescing. Mrs. M took on this role because she had once been a nurse there. She used to pass the log house on her way to her job as head nurse at the Albuquerque Sanitarium.

She told a suitor that if he bought the house, she would marry him. Arthur B. Hall bought the house in 1920, and she married him. She brought the house through periods of extensive remodeling and interior style changes. In 1930 she was divorced from A.B. Hall. By 1935, she was remarried to Herbert McCallum, (how she became known as Mrs. M.), but this marriage too would end in divorce in 1938.

The Highland Park log house was a showplace during the forties and fifties. Mrs. M spent a great deal on her house and its surroundings. She opened her home to many people, among them William Lovelace, who brought his international guests to view the house. The Mayo brothers, whose clinic is known worldwide, were frequent visitors. Governor Clyde Tingley and U.S. Senator Clinton Anderson were also friends and visitors to the house.

In 1960 she sold the house. The Albuquerque Press Club purchased the Whittlesey House in the 1970s.

ALBUQUERQUE PRESS CLUB
201 HIGHLAND PARK CIRCLE SE

# Dallas/Fort Worth, Texas

Dallas County was named after George Mifflin Dallas, who was then Vice-President of the United States. At least, that's what most people think; there are other theories as to where the name comes from. The town that became the city of Dallas was founded by John Neely Bryan in 1841. Near-by Fort Worth was founded as a military camp in 1849; it has been called "Cowtown," because of its cowboy roots.

Today, the Dallas/Fort Worth Metroplex is the fifth-largest metropolitan area in the United States. The area not only has lots of people, it has lots of ghosts.

## Runaway Bride: Jilted On Her Wedding Day, Woman in White Haunts Dallas Landmark

The Hotel Adolphus is a downtown Dallas landmark and a plush first-class hotel. But though the crowd is a posh and lively one, there's a spooky bunch there as well.

Locals say that a bride, who after being left at the altar, took her own life, marches through the hotel in her wedding finest; she also rearranges beer bottles in the hotel bar. But, hotel workers say that, fortunately, she seems to be a playful spirit—she rearranges the bottles, they move them back, minutes later she's moved them again.

In the middle of the night, hotel guests have reported seeing and hearing her walking the halls. Sometimes she is heard playing piano music, playing Big Band tunes, part of the American songbook that she favors. Typically, this happens on the nineteenth floor, which used to the location for the hotel's ballroom, and now has been remodeled into guest rooms. Most likely it was the locale where the young bride-to-be envisioned dancing the night away after her nuptials. Better late than never, seems to be her motto these days.

Since it opened in 1912, the Adolphus has maintained a reputation for lavish comfort and excellent service. But hotel guests and employees have reported numerous instances of unexplained activity throughout the building. They've reluctantly attributed the incidents to the ghosts of visitors from long ago. Many guests say they feel like someone is watching them and say they hear doors slamming in hallways where no one is walking in our out of their rooms.

In more recent years, a second female ghost has made her appearance. She was a regular visitor at the hotel, but following her death, staff says her image keeps appearing, as she takes a place at her favorite table in front of the Bistro's seating area.

In another incident, a housekeeper claimed an unseen visitor repeatedly tapped her on the shoulder as she was attempting to clean one of the hotel's restrooms. At least two hotel employees have reported windows suddenly opening and a cold blast of air rushes through the room. Mostly though, guests and hotel staff report seeing the bride. Sometimes, when she's not dancing or playing the piano, they sadly hear her crying.

Whether the Adolphus Hotel ghost stories are tall tales or not, visitors and hotel management agree the paranormal phenomena is all part of the Dallas institution's intriguing character.

HOTEL ALDOLPHUS
1321 COMMERCE STREET
DALLAS, TEXAS

## Ghosts of Cowboy Days Continue to Roam the Range of Fort Worth's Historical District

No question, Bonnie and Clyde's stay at the Stockyards Hotel in Fort Worth, Texas certainly brought fame – and stolen fortune- to storytelling about the town's historical district. But when tour guides want to corral excitement and interest about this quintessential Western establishment, they talk ghosts.

The Stockyards Hotel once housed the notorious bank robbers, and today it is home to their spirits, who are the most famous ghosts in Fort Worth. Guests report they feel, but do not see, uninvited visitors in Room 305, the room where Bonnie Parker and Clyde Barrow stayed.

Guests and hotel housekeepers report that the room gets very cold unexpectedly, then it is suddenly back to normal. They say they hear footsteps walking around the room in the middle of the night, waking them up when they're trying to sleep. Some even say that a ghostly presence has crawled into the bed with them. Water in the sink mysteriously starts flowing and they've seen a woman in period clothing, thought to be Bonnie, looking at them through the mirror over the sink.

The story is that Clyde Barrow and Bonnie visited in 1932, and, in their quick exit from the hotel (with lawmen hot on their tail), they left behind newspaper clippings, a poem written by Bonnie, which is now posted on the wall, and a revolver that was owned by Bonnie.

Col. Thomas Marion Thannisch, one of Fort Worth's early developers, built the three-story Stockyards Hotel in 1907. Over the years, it has been known as the Chandler Hotel and the Plaza Hotel, but, after its 1984 restoration, it is known as the Stockyards Hotel again.

Now restored to its original splendor, the Stockyards Hotel is certainly the hub of the ghostly goings on. Its lobby is decorated in what managers call "Cattle Baron Baroque," and includes a saloon with sports saddles for bar stools.

Beyond the ghosts that haunt Bonnie and Clyde's room, guests report ghosts in several other rooms there. And, like the entire Fort Worth Stockyards Historical District, the sounds of saloon singers, moving cattle, and jingling spurs still echo through the walls of the hotel and along the establishments on Exchange Avenue. These are ghosts of the cowboy times, claim the locals.

Nearby, the Cattlemen's Steak House is known for its beef. Patrons usually leave with full stomachs, but some also report having seen a ghostly male figure in period clothing hovering in the air and mingling from table to table. There is a photograph of a sighting that is used by restaurant owners and local ghost hunters to prove positive the historical district's ghostly goings-on.

The Cantina Cadillac nightclub and bar, the Maverick General Store, and the Stock Exchange building also are home to ghosts. Visitors say they have seen a little girl standing in a window of the

Stock Exchange building. Legend has it that the girl died after she became lost in the building and was trapped inside a vault.

There's also the Swift meatpacking plant, where ghost explorers have reported sightings of a ghostly woman and man. There are also non-automatic toilets that flush themselves. The big now-empty building at the east end of Exchange is private property and off-limits to investigators. The former meatpacking plant, which had become a restaurant, but is now boarded-up, is said to have three ghostly inhabitants.

The Stockyards Historical District area grew as a satellite of Old Fort Worth, located two and one half miles to the north. Fort Worth was settled in 1849 as an outpost along the Trinity River. It became a stop for cowboys driving cattle from South Texas along the Chisholm Trail.

By 1876, rail lines that extended from downtown Fort Worth included the Fort Worth Stockyards Belt Railway, which moved livestock from the Stockyards area to the packing plants. With Swift and Armour, the nation's two largest meatpacking companies, the area was the second-largest stockyard in the country, and headquarters of several agricultural companies.

The Stockyards Historical District is on the National Register of Historic Places.

THE STOCKYARDS HOTEL
109 EAST EXCHANGE AVENUE
THE STOCKYARDS HISTORICAL DISTRICT
FORT WORTH, TEXAS

## Playful Ghosts On the Menu at this Southern Plantation and Eatery

Knocks on the walls, slamming doors, the aroma of roses wafting through the dining room, and flying cups and saucers may scare away some of the diners at the Catfish Plantation in the historic town of Waxahachie, Texas, just outside Dallas, Texas.

But, owners Tom and Melissa Baker urge visitors not to be afraid. Instead, they insist patrons relax and enjoy the added ghostly attractions. After all, what are a few cold spots, random napkins floating across the table, and soft touches on the arm, they say. The ghosts, according to the Bakers, are as friendly as Casper.

Ghosts have visited the Catfish Plantation restaurant, housed in an 1895 Victorian home, since it opened in 1984. The ghostly goings-on have shined a national spotlight on the place, with feature stories on the phenomenon on all the major television networks in the U.S. and South America. The restaurant has received both national and worldwide acclaim and an avalanche of media attention.

Of course, the Cajun-style Catfish Plantation also is know for its food and Southern hospitality, rated three stars, and recognized as one of the outstanding rural restaurants in Texas. The atmosphere provides the true down-home Southern charm of a bygone era.

But, cuisine aside, what's behind the hauntings and unexplainable events is a question the Bakers have been asking themselves since the day they opened. On one of the first mornings, they found clean coffee cups stacked inside the large tea urn that had been mysteriously placed on the floor.

Sometimes fresh pots of coffee are found, even when no one claims to have brewed them. Chefs and kitchen staff report levitating dishes floating throughout the kitchen. Clocks reset themselves to different times, mysterious noises are heard and even the local police admit there is something very strange going on.

So concerned about the ghost phenomenon, the Bakers brought in a team of parapsychologists who, after a lengthy investigation, determined there were two female ghosts and one male ghost abiding in the Catfish Plantation. Further research suggested that the ghosts are the spirits of three former residents of the Plantation: Will, Caroline and Elizabeth.

Will was a depression-era farmer who died in the house in the 1930s. These days, he likes to sit on the front porch in his overalls. Yet, when people greet him and walk toward him, he disappears.

Caroline is said to be the liveliest spirit at the Catfish Plantation, but also the least friendly of the trio. According to the research, she lived in the house with her husband and family up to 1970. She's not too fond of all the visitors. She usually appears in the kitchen, and is said to be the cause of flying objects. Fortunately, she rarely ventures into the dining room. The food that appears to fly out of nowhere, hitting kitchen employees, is said to be thrown by Caroline when she becomes angry and frustrated because of all the strangers in her house.

The third ghost is Elizabeth, the daughter of the farmer who built the house and is most often seen in her wedding dress. She was strangled in the house on the day of her wedding, around 1920, in the area that is now the ladies' restroom. Either her ex-boyfriend or an old girlfriend of her husband-to-be reportedly committed the murder.

The scent of roses, and spots of cold air are said to be caused by Elizabeth's presence; her spectral appearance is seen in the dining room where she sometimes likes to reach out and touch the diners.

Elizabeth made her first appearance during a séance held in the dining room, which was led by a local psychic. There was knocking on the walls, dishes rattling in the kitchen, and the lit candle in the middle of the table came up "like an explosion of light." Then, the kitchen door flew open with a bang, and a young woman, dressed in an old-style wedding gown, floated into the room. The psychic identified her as Elizabeth.

These days, visitors to the Catfish Plantation can expect to be told a little about the ghosts and forewarned that their appearances might be part of the culinary experience. A sign at the entrance of the restaurant states: "If you have a ghostly experience, please tell us!"

THE CATFISH PLANTATION
814 WATER STREET
WAXAHATCHIE, TEXAS

# Denver, Colorado

Denver is located on high rolling plains, just east of the foothills of the Rocky Mountains. Denver was born during the gold rush of 1859, and its first permanent structure was a saloon. During the boomtown days of the late nineteenth century, every outlaw, lawman, and desperado in the West made a visit to the saloons and gambling halls of the Mile High City.

Today, Denver is a regional capital of the West. And, it's a boomtown again—Metro Denver is one of the fastest-growing areas in the country.

## The Unsinkable Molly Brown

In 1894, Margaret Tobin Brown, later known as The Titanic's "Unsinkable Molly Brown", left the Colorado mountain town of Leadville to live in Denver. Striving to be a part of high society, she convinced her husband, JJ Brown, a well-to-do mining engineer, that

Denver's Capitol Hill neighborhood was "the place to be." They bought their grand Victorian mansion at 1340 Pennsylvania Street for the grand sum of $30,000.

Rumors have long persisted that their spirits still haunt the house today.

With a rugged stone facade, complimented by smooth red sandstone, the lavish house also boasted stained glass windows, ornamental wood, and all of the modern technology of the day including electricity, indoor plumbing, steam heat, and telephone lines.

Having little taste for the extravagant social life his wife craved, JJ and Molly grew apart over the years. At parties, he would often drift into another room to quietly smoke a cigar. In 1920, they finally separated and two years later, he died of heart failure. Molly died ten years later, in New York City.

Over the years, the house fell into disrepair and was altered dramatically to create twelve separate spaces for roomers. For many years, it was used as a home for wayward girls.

Years later, disheartened by the state of the house and the surrounding neighborhood, the owner, Art Leisenring, and a group of concerned citizens made a grass roots effort to save the Molly Brown House from demolition. In 1971, through massive fund raising efforts, Historic Denver, Inc. was able to purchase the house for $80,000 and begin restoration. Through microscopic paint analysis, architectural research, and studying original house photographs from 1910, the house was finally restored to its original splendor.

Today, 40,000 people visit the Molly Brown House Museum each year to learn about the lifestyle enjoyed by Victorian Denver's upper classes and to gain a glimpse into the life of Denver's "unsinkable" lady. Others come hoping to witness some of the chilling paranormal activity experienced in the house by employees, volunteers, psychics and mediums.

Many report smelling the unmistakable waft of cigar smoke, despite a strict non-smoking policy. Could this be J.J enjoying a smoke in the afterlife?

Recently, a volunteer checking her hat in the hall mirror noticed a "grumpy" looking butler walking down the stairs. On another occasion, while setting the table for a Victorian dining event, another volunteer noticed a chair pushed back and the apparition of a woman in Victorian costume sitting in it.

Other reported activity includes dark shadows moving about rooms when there is no light to produce them, female voices, and piano keys moving on their own, but making no sounds. Molly's bedroom in particular has taken on a legendary status as a haunted room. Many visitors report feeling cold spots. Others will not set foot in it.

MOLLY BROWN HOUSE MUSEUM
1340 PENNSYLVANIA STREET

## A Spirited and Pricey Drink

The Oxford Hotel, a historic jewel in Denver's Lower Downtown (LoDo) district since 1891, has long had a reputation for having a number of unregistered guests.

Originally constructed in 1891 by Colorado's leading architect,

Frank E. Edbrooke, this five-story brick structure is the oldest operating hotel in Denver.

During the 1930s, Denver architect Charles Jaka remodeled the Oxford once again, transforming it to an art deco showcase. In the Cruise Room cocktail lounge, Denverites celebrated the repeal of the Prohibition Amendment.

During the war years, troop trains arriving at Union Station across the street helped to fill the Oxford to its attic and broom closets. Mothers of Denver servicemen served coffee, doughnuts and hot turkey sandwiches to the troops 24 hours a day.

After World War II ended, Denver began its second boom, emerging as a national center for federal offices, energy firms, and tourism. The Sunbelt boom town began rebuilding its downtown, demolishing many landmarks and practically all of its nineteenth-century hotels. The Oxford survived as a bastion of respectability in declining lower downtown.

Now a restored landmark and placed on the National Register of Historic Places, today's guests come to enjoy a piece of Colorado history. For those with an appetite for ghost stories, it might be an opportunity to catch a glimpse of some of Denver's unsettled spirits from these bygone times.

Legend has it you can hear what sounds like someone walking in cowboy spurs down the hallway late at night. In the late 1800s, a wealthy cowboy from California was robbed and murdered on the same floor.

In the Oxford Annex, three members of the cleaning crew saw a woman in a white dress come right through a locked door. Others have seen her float down the grand staircase. The employees of the Oxford Spa, which is located in the former front desk check-in for the Annex, also are certain her spirit remains.

It is reported that Room 320 is the most haunted room of them all: it is where a love triangle ended tragically. In the early 1900s a mistress committed suicide because her married lover never returned. There have been strange noises and sightings reported in that room for over 100 years. Visitors are said to have seen the faint image of a woman standing in the room. Others have captured on film what appears to be a woman's face.

The hotel's Cruise Room bar, which saw big business during World War II from countless trains through Union Station, has seen its share of ghosts. During a busy night at the bar recently, a bartender noticed a man, dressed in a train conductor's uniform, walk in and sit down at the back booth, facing the wall-to-wall crowd.

He asked how much the beer was and when told "$4.25," he said, "Boy, beer sure costs more now." Witnesses saw him slowly sip the beer from the bottle. A short while later, he disappeared. He hadn't walked out, because the crowd would have seen him push through to the exit. Inquiring wait staff went to the booth, picked up the beer and found that not a drop was gone.

THE OXFORD HOTEL
1600 17th STREET

## Ghostly Callings

Built in 1892, the Brown Palace has played host to presidents, kings, tycoons and celebrities. Like the Oxford Hotel, it was designed by Colorado's famed architect, Frank Edbrooke. Its triangular shape, in an opulent Italian Renaissance style, allows every guestroom to be washed in sunlight at some point during each day. Inside, the eight-story atrium lobby is worthy of an Edith Wharton novel, with an abundance of burnished wood, wainscoting made of Mexican onyx, a grand staircase and a stained glass ceiling.

Mediums and paranormal experts love to check in to the Brown Palace Hotel.

For over a hundred years, claims of ghostly encounters and sightings have been exchanged. Although many assume that these involve its most famous guests, like Augusta Tabor, married to Colorado's famous Silver King, or "the Unsinkable Molly Brown", sources at the hotel claim they do not. Rather, they say, these are the ghostly echoes of some of the ordinary people who, for some reason, have chosen to linger.

Through the years, The Brown Palace has seen it all - boom times and depressions, peace and war. If the walls could talk, they would tell of love and betrayal, success and failure, happiness and despair. Perhaps these spirits are trying to tell their stories. Of the many reports, here are just a few:

There are common reports of feminine laughter and chatter in the eighth floor hallway, outside present day Room 801, which was originally part of the ballroom. One can imagine these to be Victorian young women en route to powder their noses, giggling about the eligible men who'd escorted them to the ball.

Recent sightings by hotel employees have involved a spirit in uniform. He has been seen outside the Brown Palace Club in a conductor's uniform. The hotel originally housed the ticket office for the Rock Island Railroad, so it seems plausible that a mortal conductor might have once walked the halls. When sighted, this spirit simply disappears through the walls.

On another occasion, a bellman delivering newspapers to the upper floor rooms found some of the papers missing from his cart. A few minutes later he encountered an apparition dressed in old-fashioned uniform. He was so frightened that he quit the next day.

A maintenance man was recently called to Room 523, in which the guest complained that the room was too hot. He was met at the door by a pale, old woman wearing a long, flowing black gown. When he'd adjusted the controls, he turned to tell her everything was fine, but she was nowhere to be seen. He called the front desk to report that the job was complete, and could they please let the guest know when she returned. There was a long pause before the desk clerk answered, "That room is unoccupied."

Prior to the main dining room being renamed Ellygton's, the restaurant was known as the San Marco Room, and was home to big bands, and later, the San Marco Strings. One night, a houseman went to investigate sounds coming from the dining room. Upon entering, he discovered a quartet of formally dressed musicians, practicing their music. As it was long past closing time, the irritated houseman said, "You're not supposed to be in here." They replied, "Oh don't worry about us. We live here."

The most sophisticated prank of all was played by the ghost of a woman who lived and died in a suite on the ninth floor. Mrs. Crawford Hill was the undisputed queen of Denver society. Her glamorous life story ended with heartbreak, resulting in her living at the hotel for the last fifteen years of her life. As part of a "lovers and scandals" tour of the hotel, the historian began to include her story. After these new tours first began, the switchboard was inundated with calls from her former room. When answered, there was only static. What was happening? An extensive renovation was underway on the ninth floor, and her old apartment was empty. It had been stripped of furniture, carpeting, wallpaper, lights, and telephones.

When Mrs. Hill's saga was dropped from subsequent tours, the calls ceased.

THE BROWN PALACE HOTEL
321 17th STREET

# Houston, Texas

Houston is the fourth-largest city in the United States; it is named for Sam Houston, the former president of the Republic of Texas and the first governor of the state of Texas.

Houston is the capital of the American energy (think oil) and aeronautics (think Mission Control) industries. And, the Port of Houston is the sixth-largest port in the world.

## A Boy and His Dog Make This Houston Cemetery a Spooky Place

These days, it is a private cemetery on private land. But ghosts are persistent, and so when they want to haunt, issues like private property don't seem to matter.

That's the case at the Woodlawn Cemetery in Houston, Texas. Privately owned and managed by a Houston family, it continues to be an intriguing location for ghost hunters. Even though they operate from outside the gates.

Woodlawn Cemetery is a charming, mostly modern cemetery. But, at Woodlawn, there are several ghosts, including one that barks.

There's the ghost who appears at the grave of Johnny Morehouse. According to legend, he and his dog are the top ghost dogs, so to speak, at the cemetery. Johnny is the ghost of a little five-year-old boy who fell into the Miami and Erie Canal and froze to death, even though his dog was trying to rescue him. When he was buried, the poor dog lay on his gravesite and wouldn't leave. Eventually, the dog died of starvation and dehydration. The owners of the cemetery at the time created a tombstone for the dog.

Today, the boy and his best canine friend are reported to roam the cemetery, especially after-hours. People–from outside the cemetery gates—hear barking near Johnny's grave and they even have seen images, which suddenly disappear, of a boy and a dog.

Another Woodlawn Cemetery ghost is a pretty blonde girl in jeans and white tennis shoes who sits on a stone and occasionally talks to passersby, who usually fail to realize she isn't a real person until later. No one knows exactly why her spirit is restless, but it's theorized that she is unhappy because she's not buried near her father.

Woodlawn is also said to be home to the ghost of a Russian ballerina, who is entombed in one of the family mausoleums. Her likeness is carved into the wall of the mausoleum. On nights with full moons, it is said, you can see her dancing outside her final resting-place.

Woodlawn Cemetery can be visited during the day, and, even during the day, orbs have been seen.

WOODLAWN CEMETERY
NORTHWEST HOUSTON
(Please note: this is a private cemetery on private land.)

# Las Vegas, Nevada

Las Vegas started as a tent town in 1904 when the Union Pacific Railroad decided it would make a good stop-off for the railroad. Soon saloons, stores, and boarding houses cropped up. Gambling was legalized by the Nevada state legislature in 1931, for the purpose of raising money for public schools. Today, gambling revenues account for 43% of the state's general budget.

## It's Not Just the Las Vegas Strip That Lights Up

Most people know that there are ghost towns in old Nevada, but not every one knows that the state's largest and liveliest city, Las Vegas—famous for greed, gambling, and fun—would create such an atmosphere for ghostly hauntings. But, it's an unusual but normal part of a casino employee's workday to encounter the friendly and sometimes unfriendly spirits that reside in the city of all-night neon lights.

The spirits served up on the strip are not all of the liquid kind.

Many a ghost tour will take you by the glitzy, famous hotels and casinos, spin the ghostly stories of greed, sex, murder, and, of course, Elvis sightings. But, if you work in one of the hotels on the Strip, ghostly encounters could be a normal part of your workday. The friendly and sometimes unfriendly spirits that reside in the city of neon lights are your colleagues. There are numerous strange noises, bathroom faucets turning off and on, lights flickering, mysterious footsteps, and eerie feelings of being followed and watched.

The Tropicana has its weird history of the Tiki Mask greeter. Guests at the hotel have been greeted by a man in a large purple tiki mask. Some have had their photos taken with him, but when they are developed, the mask appears as a strange hazy purple cloud.

Has Elvis left the building? The ghost of Elvis Presley, in his white sequined jumpsuit, has been spotted by stagehands and even Wayne Newton himself at the Las Vegas Hilton, once the International Hotel, where the King had made a comeback in 1969.

The Bally's Hotel and Casino is now located on the site of the old MGM Hotel where a terrible fire killed 84 people in 1980. Employees and guests have seen glowing orbs and apparitions in the halls.

The Luxor Hotel, with its pyramid design has had its share of unfortunate incidents. Two construction workers died during the construction, and others were injured. Some believe that the secret properties of a pyramid shape do not belong on the strip. A psychic suggested that an artificial eye needs to be placed at the capstone of the pyramid to prevent any bad luck from happening.There is a sense that the Luxor is haunted but, we do not know details.

There is also the sense that the Excaliber is haunted, but by whom we do not know. Customers have said that they feel they are not alone on the elevators, even when they are.

Bathroom spirits seem to favor haunting Caesar's Palace and the

Mirage. In both of these hotels, there are sensory faucets that go off and on when nobody is there.

The ghost of gangster Bugsy Siegel is said to haunt the Flamingo Hilton Hotel. The development of Las Vegas was a dream, even an obsession, of his. He was the owner of the original Flamingo. His specter has been seen by many of the guests who stay in the Presidential Suite. He is most often sighted wearing his smoking jacket near the bathroom, which he helped decorate. He is very proud of it; his choice of green fixtures are still there. Mr. Ben Siegel's ghost is also known to favor sitting by the hotel's pool late at night.

Bugsy Siegel loved the Flamingo Hotel as he loved the whole idea of Las Vegas—a gambling oasis in the middle of the desert. He wanted the hotel to be extravagant, and he did everything in his power to convince the bosses that there was a great future in Las Vegas. Unfortunately for Bugsy, the Flamingo was a little slow to catch on, and his bosses decided it was time for him to go. He was gunned down at Virginia Hill's home in June 1947, at the young age of 41. He didn't live to see the incredible Las Vegas of his dreams, at least not while he was alive, but his spirit is another story.

Las Vegas is certainly a very lively, exciting city—even the dead stay up here.

THE LAS VEGAS STRIP
LAS VEGAS BOULEVARD

Haunted Vegas Tour Las Vegas
305 Convention Center
Las Vegas, Nevada
89109
1-800-591-6423

# Phoenix, Arizona

Phoenix was a settlement founded on the ruins of the Pueblo Grande civilization and its impressive centuries-old network of irrigation canals that brought water from the Salt River. The name Phoenix was chosen, inasmuch as the new town would spring from the ruins of the former civilization.

## Some Like it Hot: Scorned Lover Continues to Haunt Hotel San Carlos

The Hotel San Carlos in downtown Phoenix is a popular stop for Southwestern tourists. It's definitely a hot spot. But, the steaming 110-degree summer weather isn't the only thing that keeps the place hot.

The hotel is said to be haunted by the ghost of a young 22-year-old woman who, brokenhearted over the end of her relationship with a hotel bellboy, jumped off the roof of the seven-story building, taking her life. That was on May 7, 1928, and the haunting began shortly thereafter.

Even today, the ghost of 22-year-old Leone Jensen creates strange blasts of cold and hot air throughout the hotel. Guests report seeing a misty image of a young woman in a white evening gown traipsing through the halls, but all of a sudden she disappears. People have taken photographs where a white cloud appears.

And, Leone's ghost is not alone. The sounds of children laughing also light up the hallways, perhaps the spirits of children who long ago played on the playground of the city's original schoolyard.

Indeed, The Hotel San Carlos is steeped in rich history. It rests on the site of the first school in Phoenix. The sound of children laughing and playing is often heard, even when there are no children checked in at the hotel. One guest wrote about seeing three children running down the hall on the second floor and suddenly disappearing as they turn the corner.

Some say one reason the hotel is haunted might be an old water well in the basement that is still being used. The well, dug for a school that was built in 1874, tapped into a spring that was considered sacred for hundreds of years. Native Americans worshiped on this spot long before the school or the hotel were built.

Today, the San Carlos is said to be one of the most haunted hotels in America. This historic 121-room hotel is located in a 1928 Italian Renaissance-style building, and has hosted celebrities such as Clark Gable, Spencer Tracy, and Mae West (who has a suite named after her).

Local ghost busters have collaborated the stories about this young woman ghost. They say even the architecture and style of the hotel makes it a ripe stomping ground for ghosts. When some ghost hunters have tried to take pictures of the orbs that they can see, their cameras often break or run out of batteries. But, some pictures have been taken. When they are developed or downloaded, orbs mysteriously appear in the pictures.

Antique oil paintings adorn the walls, and red velvet chairs are scattered across the lobby. A worn journal that lies on the front desk in the lobby chronicles some of the guest's unexplained experiences. According to some reports, Leone Jensen has been getting bolder in recent years; on occasion, she has even appeared at the foot of guest's beds. She has a special interest in the top floor, the floor that leads to the roof.

HOTEL SAN CARLOS
202 NORTH CENTRAL AVENUE

# Salt Lake City, Utah

Nestled in a valley between Utah's Great Salt Lake and the Wasatch Mountains, Salt Lake City has its share of paranormal phenomena: lake monsters, ghosts, Bigfoot, UFOs, mystery spots and mystic visions.

Many attribute all the paranormal activity to the fact that Salt Lake City is rich in mystic and spiritual experience. It was founded in 1847 by a group of pioneers led by Brigham Young, leader of the Church of Jesus Christ of Latter-Day Saints, better known as the Mormons. They came to Salt Lake City for refuge from persecution and ridicule. Today, the valley remains the headquarters of the church.

Perhaps because the founding of the religion is steeped in mysticism, miracles and visions, the town seems to have no shortage of ghosts. There's even a Utah Ghost Organization to chronicle the numerous spottings.

## When the Curtain Goes Up, The Ghosts Perform

The Capitol Theater in downtown Salt Lake City is the site of several ghost stories.

According to one story, an usher named "George" was killed there in a fire in the 1940's. Ever since then, lights switch on an off, doors lock and unlock themselves, toilets flush unattended, and there's even a Coke machine that exhibits strange behavior. The elevator takes you to floors that you didn't push the button.

Located in the heart of downtown Salt Lake City, this historic landmark is the home of Ballet West, the Utah Opera, and the Ririe-Woodbury Dance Company. The theater also hosts touring Broadway productions and community arts education programs. When it was built in 1913, the building was called the Orpheum Theatre, and it featured some of the "highest standard acts and greatest stars of the stage."

During its early days, vaudevillians entertained crowds twice daily; vaudeville continued to reign as king-of-the-house and movies provided a sideline.

The theatre was sold in 1927 to Louis Marcus, a much-respected mayor of Salt Lake City and Utah movie pioneer. Marcus enlarged the seating capacity to 2,260, installed the Wurlitzer with the well-respected Alexander Schreiner as its spotlighted musician. The theater also had a new name, the Capitol Theater.

After an eight-million-dollar facelift in the 1970s, it reopened in 1978. It is part of the Salt Lake County Center for the Arts.

CAPITOL THEATRE
50 WEST 200 SOUTH

## Ghosts Are Kidding Around at Salt Lake City and County Building

It is a building that governs Utah with the serious matters of politics. But behind the scenes at the Old City and County Building in Salt Lake City, ghosts are kidding around all the time. Literally.

That's because two of the ghosts that haunt the 1893 building are the apparitions of children. And, of course, they like to play. They run around up and down stairs on the higher floors, changing the thermostats, slamming doors, turning lights on and off, and laughing without seemingly a care in the world. Remember, after all, they are ghosts.

Their ghostly presence makes good conversation for building security officers who admit to feeling scared at times, especially at night on the fifth floor. Security officers also claim to have been grabbed by these ghostly kids and often hear them running around, playing and laughing. The children are said to be a brother and sister, who were killed when the structure was being built. It is said that there is still another ghost who is their mother.

The downtown building has been investigated numerous times by local ghost hunting groups. They say they also sometimes hear the "step, clump" of a former judge with a wooden leg, the "click, whoosh" of a woman in high heels wearing a long skirt, as well as the sounds of these children playing.

The building houses the seat of city government and is on

Washington Square, at the spot where the original Mormon settlers circled their wagons on their first night in the Salt Lake Valley. It is said to be modeled after London's City Hall and it has details common to the Romanesque Revival style. Construction began in 1892 and continued for two years. After Utah achieved statehood in 1896, the building served as the capitol for nineteen years until the current capitol building was finished.

The City and County Building is an architectural masterpiece. The Utah Heritage Foundation provides tours of the City & County Building on Tuesdays and Saturdays. Tours typically last about an hour.

CITY AND COUNTY BUILDING
451 SOUTH STATE STREET

## Desperate Housewife Returns to Haunt

It's been called the most haunted house in Utah. Visitors, who are escorted by ghost hunters, hear the voices of children, phantom footsteps, doorknobs rattling; they report seeing ghostly images and stationary objects moving.

That's just a small part of the paranormal activity at Brigham Young's Forest Farm House. Located in the Place Heritage Park, the old farmhouse was one of the homes of Brigham Young, the leader of the Mormon Church after its founder Joseph Smith was killed in 1844. It's been opened for the first time in years to be part of a circuit of haunted house tours in Utah.

The Mormons created Utah, escaping from religious persecution in the late 1840s. With all of the bloodshed and violence that accompanied their travels and western settlement, it is obvious that they would leave behind a legacy of ghosts.

Today, forest preserve employees and visitors have reported many spooky goings-on in the farmhouse. One of the ghosts is said to be that of a young 19-year-old woman, who was murdered on her way to Salt Lake City; the eerie setting of the old farmhouse is where her spirit chose to reside.

Another ghost at the farmhouse is said to be Ann Eliza Webb, the nineteenth wife of Brigham Young. But, Ann was a strong-minded woman; after her brief time as Young's wife, she got a divorce and began denouncing Mormonism on the lecture circuit. She even published a book: *Wife No. 19: The Story of a Life in Bondage.*

Ghost hunters say she returns to the house to continue to vocalize her opposition to Brigham Young. They say they have seen Ann, especially in the dining room. She is a petite woman, and is dressed in black. Sometimes they can even smell her cooking (when there's nothing on the stove). She loved to cook in life, so she continues to prepare food in the kitchen and eat in the dining room in her death.

FOREST FARM HOUSE
OLD DESERET
PIONEER STATE PARK

# San Antonio, Texas

In 1691, a group of Spanish explorers and missionaries came upon what is now the San Antonio River on the feast day of St. Anthony, hence naming the river after the saint. Today, it is a thriving metropolis with a population of more than one million people.

## Castle Captures Imagination and Ghostly Happenings at this Bed and Breakfast

San Antonio, Texas may be known for The Alamo and the first settlers who appeared on the muddy banks of the San Antonio River nearly three centuries ago. And, the city certainly has seen more than its share of gunfights, revolutions, and crimes of passion.

So it's no wonder that a few–actually many–spirits wander the concrete canyons of the original part of downtown. In fact, some professional ghost hunters say there is no five acres more haunted than that surrounding the site of the Alamo. It has been said that San Antonio is one of the hottest spots in the nation for paranormal occurrences.

That may be because thousands of Native Americans were buried, but maybe not laid to rest, in the cemetery next to the mission known as the Alamo.

So, it's no surprise then that the historic Terrell Castle Bed & Breakfast, just miles away from the Alamo, is one of the most haunted places in town. Located in the historic Government Hill District, Terrell Castle is a popular tourist stop, a great place to sleep and eat.

But, guests report numerous "interesting" occurrences. Footsteps that sound like a woman in high-heeled shoes are heard on the stairs. But no one is there.

Toilet seats have been known to slam down at regular, thirty-minute intervals, but when hotel maintenance examines the situation, there appears to be no problem. Ceiling fans spin when the switch is turned off. Televisions literally jump off their stands in guest rooms. Members of the housekeeping staff report seeing a shadow of someone walking down the hall. But, there's no one there.

Terrell Castle was built in 1894 as the residence of Edwin Holland Terrell. Mr. Terrell was a lawyer and statesman who served as Ambassador to Belgium during the presidency of Benjamin Harrison in the early 1890's. While in Europe, Terrell fell in love with the castles and chateaus of Belgium and France. Upon his return to Texas, he commissioned an architect, Alfred Giles, to design this home, patterned after those castles in Europe. It was to be a "castle for his bride" and their six children. The Terrell family lived here until Edwin's death in 1910. It has had a succession of owners since then, and has been operating as a bed and breakfast since 1986. One critic described it as "the most elegant Bed and Breakfast in Texas."

TERRELL CASTLE BED & BREAKFAST
950 EAST GRAYSON STREET

## Remember the Alamo: How could you NOT, with all of these ghosts?

Construction of Misión San Antonio de Valero, the mission that became famous as the Alamo, began on the present site in 1724. In the early 1800s, the Alamo was first used as a military post by the Spanish cavalry.

During the famous siege of March 1836, at the time of the Texas War of Independence, nearly two hundred defenders of the Alamo, led by Colonel William Travis, lost their lives—among them were Davy Crockett and Jim Bowie. More than one thousand Mexican soldiers, led by General Antonio Lopez de Santa Anna, also lost their lives in the battle. Few received proper burial; bodies were buried in mass graves, thrown into the San Antonio River, or incinerated in mounds.

It's no wonder the site of the Alamo is one that is rife with reportings of ghosts. Today this mission-turned-fortress-turned national museum is infested with the spirits of the men who fought here. Many visitors say they are overwhelmed by feelings of sadness; others say they feel as if they actually know the souls they are crying for, as if their spirits touched them during their visit. Sightseers encounter cold and hot spots.

And, then there are the ghosts that visitors see. One of the most-repeated stories of an Alamo ghost is the story of a small blonde-haired boy ghost that is seen from time to time in the left upstairs window of the Alamo mission house, now the gift shop. According to legend, the little boy may have been evacuated during the siege and perhaps returns again and again to the place where he last saw his relatives. Though he is seen year-round, he is usually seen each February, the month the siege began.

Some of the Federal Marshals and other staff who work at the Alamo today are afraid to go in the basement. Some had such frightening experiences that they have quit their jobs—because of the toll of the ghosts who haunt nearly every building within the block.

Today, the Alamo is dedicated as a national shrine and museum. But few people, who grew up with the Davy Crockett-Hollywood version of The Alamo, realize it is one of the most haunted locales in America.

The Alamo monument and museum are memorials to the defenders of the Alamo. Today, the Alamo is a symbol of a heroic struggle against overwhelming odds, and is a Shrine to Texas Liberty.

THE ALAMO
300 ALAMO PLAZA

# The West Coast

In the Georgetown area of Seattle is a Victorian house, built over a hundred years ago and now a private residence. This particular house has quite a history of paranormal activity. Jake knows from conversations with previous owners that the house is haunted.

In San Francisco, tourists at Fisherman's Wharf can meet sea lions, sample delicious local seafood, take the ferry to Alcatraz Island, and then travel under the Golden Gate Bridge. They'll hear all about the ghosts galore that haunt the nation's most notorious prison, but what may come as an eerie surprise is to learn about the number of folk who jump from the Golden Gate Bridge to end their lives. And, continue to haunt. Back on land, heading up to Pacific Heights, there are ghosts galore haunting the Victorian mansions, the Painted Ladies, of the city.

From the Sunset Strip to the Hollywood sign, Los Angeles is not just the City of Angels; it's also home to many ghosts. Some say they are the spirits of those who headed west for fame and fortune, and found their dreams unfulfilled. Today, they still hang around, hoping for that fame and success.

Heading down Highway 101 South, San Diego is a city ripe for ghosts. At The El Fandango Restaurant, for example, the spirit of a Victorian-era woman who once made her home there greets diners. In fact, many of the hotels, restaurants and museums in San Diego's historical district are haunted.

Tourists who head to the West Coast will find many of these places open to the public, and there's a rich offering of city tours to choose from to get a glimpse of the ghosts firsthand.

# Seattle, Washington

The following stories are from Jake who runs "The Haunted Happenings Seattle Ghosts Tours." She is a Seattle native who has had a strong interest in the paranormal all her life. She created the tours four years ago and they are available year round.

## Sleepless in Seattle: Ghosts in Georgetown

In the Georgetown area of Seattle is a particular Victorian house, built over a hundred years ago and now a private residence. This particular house has quite a history of paranormal activity. Jake knows from conversations with previous owners that the house is haunted.

In the early 1900s, a woman named Sarah came to visit her sister who lived in the house. Her brother-in-law raped her. Sarah became pregnant and when she had her baby, the brother-in-law took the baby from her and murdered the baby. After Sarah died, she returned to haunt the house, floating around the halls, whispering softly, and crying for her baby.

Two different individual owners of the house during the 1970s and 1980s told Jake that they knew the house was haunted. Both had seen Sarah roaming the house. They said that the second floor had an incredible amount of poltergeist activity. Objects were always moving, lights turning on and off, and you'd hear low whispers behind you.

In fact, when the house was empty, before the latest owners moved in in the fall of 2004, neighbors would see lit candles in the windows of the second floor front tower room. They would have to get into the house and blow them out. When the house was rented out, the property owner used to have a policy of making tenants sign a disclaimer that they were told that there was poltergeist activity in the house. Not too surprisingly, the turnover in renters was frequent.

One story about the house is that several years ago, a young man who was a painter lived there; Sarah appeared to him, and he painted her portrait. He hung it in the spot where she first appeared to him. The portrait looked exactly like the visions of Sarah other people had experienced.

Some ghosts, other than Sarah, are attributed to the time when the house was a brothel, and violent and sordid behavior often happened within the rooms of the house. One story is that of a young male tenant of the house who was emotionally troubled, and became frantic over the voices whispering in his ears, never giving him a moment's peace. He could barely make out the words, but they confused and disturbed him; sadly, the voices were so bad that it pushed him into committing suicide by jumping off of the tallest bridge in Seattle.

If you take Jake's tour, you will go by the house, which is now a private home. But, who knows how long the new owners will last with Sarah and the other restless souls still occupying this Victorian Georgetown home.

GEORGETOWN VICTORIAN HOUSE
PRIVATE RESIDENCE

## Shopping with the Spirits

Ghostly experiences are not new to the historical Pike Place Market in Seattle. Ghosts can be seen as you wonder through the shops; often groups of ghost hunters wander through the market armed with digital cameras, electromagnetic energy readers, and sound recorders.

One familiar ghost often seen, felt, and photographed is the late Market Director Arthur Goodwin. He so loved the place his ghost refuses to leave. So, if you are shopping and suddenly feel a cold spot, a mysterious push, or see a floating bolt of light, you know more than the living are enjoying the day shopping at the market.

One very haunted building in the area, a four story building, was once one of the largest funeral parlors in the city of Seattle. The basement housed the crematorium, the stables, and the horse-drawn hearses. The main floor contained the viewing rooms and chapel. Embalming was done on the top floor. This was for a long time one of the only funeral parlors for the then-young growing city, and many a dead soul passed through. And, some have decided to stay.

The building has been many things over the years, but restaurants seem to be attracted to the location. Many have opened, and many have closed; in fact, two restaurants recently opened and closed back-to-back, each lasting about eight months. The bartender in one of these restaurants told Jake about being at the bar and suddenly feeling a cold breeze. Bottles of wine went floating out from the bar, the front door opened, and the bottles landed on the street.

The property manager has many accounts of poltergeist activity. There is a phantom male sitting in a back booth, smiling and greeting customers; a woman in a long white dress, much like a funeral gown, roams the building, frequently seen by customers and employees.

A few years ago a Thai restaurant opened, calling themselves in Thai, "Funeral Flower". Once opened, they said they felt menacing spirits, saw moving objects, heard strange noises, saw doors opening and closing, and experienced spots of very cold air. They closed quickly.

The only business that has seemed to last is a pub and restaurant on the bottom floor: Kell's. They seem to have come to terms with their fellow occupiers and go about their business.

A new bar/lounge recently opened called the Starlight Lounge; they hope to also make peace with their Pike Place Ghosts.

Kell's and the Starlight Lounge are located at 1st Avenue and Stewart Street.

PIKE PLACE MARKET
PIKE PLACE & WESTERN AVENUE

## It's Chinatown, Jake

In the heart of Seattle's Chinatown, there is a building, which takes up to half of a city block, that is a former gambling den. One cold and windy winter day in February of 1983, three men devised a murderous plot that entailed robbery and death. The main man behind the plan was a 22-year old Chinese-American named Willie Mak. He worked for another gambling club, and had thousand of dollars worth of debts; he came up with a plan to steal the money from the wealthier Wah Mee Club.

From the 1920s on, the Wah Mee was a speakeasy and gambling den. The police looked the other way, even though they knew there was illegal gambling there, since they themselves profited from allowing the exclusive gambling club.

Willie Mak, with two friends, Benjamin Ng, a criminal of record, and another friend, Tony Ng (no relation to Benjamin), worked out a plan that one of them would befriend the door attendant at the club. The attendant let people in by looking at them through a peephole door; this would allow the three to gain entry into the club. Thus was the beginning of one of the worst massacres in Seattle's history.

On that fateful night, the door was opened to allow the three men access to the gambling parlor; no one was expecting the violence that would ensue. The three men took the twelve men and one woman, who were the unfortunate gamblers that night, to the basement, where they hog-tied them. As the victims lay on the cold basement floor, the robbers shot each one of them in the head, execution-style, shooting each one twice, making sure they were dead. They then proceeded to rob the establishment, taking $25,000 away with them.

There was one problem with the plan—one of the shot men lived, and because they had not been blindfolded, he saw their faces. He kept perfectly still. After they fled the scene, he freed himself from the nylon ropes and crawled out into the alleyway, where he was discovered by a passerby. The police were called. The survivor, Wai Chin, easily identified Willie Mak, Benjamin Ng, and Tony Ng.

Willie Mak and Benjamin Ng were caught hours later. Tony had fled to Calgary, Alberta, Canada, but was brought back. After their convictions, Willie Mak was sentenced to death, later reduced to life in prison, Benjamin Ng was sentenced to life in prison, and Tony Ng, convicted of robbery and assault but not murder, received seven consecutive life terms. They are all now serving their life sentences in prison.

Today the building is 80% occupied, and the gambling den area has not reopened. The owners of the building say that there is bad karma in that section of the building, and they will not rent out the location. In fact, they themselves have not entered that section of their own building since the murders took place.

There is an old Chinese belief that when you die, you go to the underground for three years, then you pick a new body to occupy. Because of this many people are leery of places where they know death has happened. The fear being that the lost souls will take over your body and spirit.

Many people walking by this building get a very strong sense of panic; fear oozes out of the building, and one feels an overwhelming sense of sadness. If you peek through the old peephole, an energy force seems to collide with your eyes, you might feel faint, perhaps gambling with your life.

The building is located on Maynard Avenue in the Chinatown International District.

MAYNARD AVENUE
CHINATOWN, SEATTLE

## A Lady in Waiting: Seattle's Leading Lady Continues to Take Center Stage

The building in which the Harvard Exit Theater resides was originally constructed for the Woman's Century Club in 1925. The club, whose members were dedicated to getting the right to vote and equality for women, continues to hold meetings in the lobby. The Harvard Exit Theater opened as a movie theater in 1968, and was run by people described as eccentric film buffs. The Landmark Theater chain took over the operations in 1979, and put in another screen on the third floor. Today, the Harvard Exit Theater specializes in art films, and is the sight of film festivals, such as the Seattle International Film Festival.

Today, the Women's Century Club meets at the theater twice a week. And legend has it, its founding members have yet to miss a meeting—at least in spirit, anyway. According to reports, the female ghosts have the want-to-be-seen attitude, appearing regularly at the theater house, which is located in the Capitol Hill section of downtown Seattle.

Indeed, since the 1970s the ghost of several women decked out in turn-of-the-century garb have been appearing regularly at the theater. The most frequent spirits include two different female ghosts who have been seen in the first-floor lobby in person and even in photos taken of the supposedly empty room. One spirit is believed to be Bertha Landis, a strong spirit in life, who was the founder of the Women's Century Club, the City Federation of Women's Clubs, and was also Seattle's first mayor. The spirit of Bertha Landis is the most common apparition spotted by the living. She seems to like to keep an eye on the place, help out the managers, and she doesn't plan to leave anytime soon.

Ghostly film enthusiasts have been known to reorganize the film canisters around the projection room, much to the annoyance of the living. On several occasions, theater managers have opened the building and found the projector showing a film to an unseen audience. In one instance, a projectionist arrived and found a movie playing to an empty, dark house. He made haste to the projection room to catch the guilty party, but the door was locked from the inside.

From its inception, Harvard Exit Theater has been described as an unusual, luxurious home, more than just a theater. The first floor main lobby is described as being grand and glorious, full of the 1920s ambiance, featuring a grand piano and a beautiful chandelier. Comfortable chairs, some with tables and lamps, are grouped around the huge fireplace, which is always traditionally lit for the patrons.

The fact that these spirits still enjoy the ambiance and atmosphere of the Harvard Exit Theater has been the topic of many newspapers and television shows, and has drawn many psychics to investigate the building with their equipment, medium contacts, and personal experiences.

HARVARD EXIT THEATER
807 ROY STREET

Haunted Happenings Seattle Ghost Tours
206-365-3739
Reservations required
www.privateeyetours.com

Jake's tours cover a large area of Seattle, visiting various locations of supernatural occurences both part and present.

She also offers two different Mystery & Murder Tours covering the darker side of Seattle.

Van tours last 2–3 Hours

Enjoy!

# Portland, Oregon

The Lewis and Clark Expedition, the arrival of the Hudson Bay Trading Company, the Oregon Trail migration, Olympic skater Tanya Harding. Certainly, Portland, Oregon has some unusual surprises tucked away for visitors. But what most don't know is that this town is also home to numerous hauntings.

## Booking It: Ghosts Peering Out of Book Shelves at the North Portland Library

The North Portland Library at the corner of North Killingsworth and North Commercial Streets is one of the most haunted places in town. Local ghost hunters say it is not surprising that there are so many ghosts in Portland. For those who understand that Portland has a dark history, the haunting spirits make a lot of sense.

The ghosts come to life at places like the library, a classic Carnegie style building with open-beamed wooden ceilings and two public meeting rooms that was built in 1913. The largest of the meeting rooms, and the haunted one, is upstairs. It is a large 150-seat second floor meeting room, which is usually closed off from the public when not in use. This is where the ghosts seem to haunt. Security cameras mounted outside and inside the room have picked up pictures of a man moving around the room. He could be, some say, the person who is directly responsible for Portland's darkest days.

That dark history began in the late 1800s with Joseph "Bunco" Kelly, an hotelier notorious for kidnapping young men and selling them to ship captains. Kelly worked the town with his unscrupulous ways and many bar owners and hotel operators were forced to rely on this Shanghai trade to keep their doors open. Kelly and his co-workers would lure intoxicated potential crewmembers and drop them off on the ships where they would then be stranded at sea and forced to work for long periods of time.

One Library assistant viewing the security monitor at the main desk noticed a man, who some believe to be Kelly, sitting in a chair in the meeting room on the second floor. Only problem was that there were no meetings, and that floor was sealed off. She brought her observation to the attention of her supervisor. After viewing it together, they went and unlocked the door to the ascending stairwell and step-by-step, they climbed until the meeting room was in view. There was nothing there; the room was completely vacant. This happens frequently—the man is spotted on the security cameras, but when security goes into the room, he is not there. This has happened several times.

Library workers say the man also haunts Commercial Street, alongside the library, heading over to Jefferson High School. This happens in the wee hours of the morning and workers say that they not only see him, they hear his footsteps. But suddenly he disappears.

In addition to Kelly, there was "Sweet Mary," the proprietor of a brothel, who also brought a dark side to Portland's history in the late nineteenth century. To elude taxes and city laws, she operated her bordello on a barge that ran up and down the Willamette River. Technically, she was outside everyone's jurisdiction. When ghost hunters spot female ghosts in the library area, they attribute the haunting to "Sweet Mary."

Portland is a city of parks, outdoor artwork, coffee carts, micro-breweries, bridges, and bookstores. Portland is a people town, whose pedestrian-friendly city blocks are half the size of those in other towns, and where limits on growth have kept the surrounding countryside within a twenty minute drive from the city's core.

It's not only a great place to live, it's a great place to be a ghost.

NORTH PORTLAND LIBRARY
512 NORTH KILLINGSWORTH STREET

## Ghosts Stir Up Excitement in University of Portland Classrooms

Nestled in the great Willamette Valley, The University of Portland is on the site of what was once a Native American settlement. Today, the university still oozes paranormal and spiritual energies, which most attribute to the psychic activity of these once sacred grounds.

One of the oldest buildings on campus is Christie Hall. Now a dormitory, students, especially those who don't leave campus during holidays and semester breaks, report many unexplainable goings-on. Most say they feel like they are being watched while in their rooms and that even though their windows may be closed, the blinds will move and a strong breeze will blast through their rooms.

Legend has it that the building's basement was once the infirmary for dying priests who lived on campus who are part of the Congregation of Holy Cross. And, that exorcisms were performed in what is now the laundry room.

Nearby in Kenna Hall, there's a ghost residing with the students. Apparently this ghost once lived in the oldest building on campus, Waldschmidt Hall, but moved into Kenna when Waldschmidt was remodeled. The University was once a boarding school, and the ghost is reported to be a young boy who drowned in the Willamette pool in the late nineteenth century.

The boy typically appears in the laundry room, decked out in dripping wet clothes. Some say his body appears bloated, almost as if he has come back from being submerged in the water.

Several other buildings on campus are also rumored to be haunted, along with the bluff that overlooks the university. The Mago Hut Theater and the University Commons, located on the south side of campus near the bluff, are also haunted.

A man named Frank Houston owned the land on the southwest side of the bluff near the Commons. No fan of the black-robed men of Holy Cross, he refused to sell his property to the congregation for a reasonable price. His widow finally sold the tract to the University in the 1930s after Houston died. Tradition has it that Frank Houston is one of the several ghosts haunting the campus; his perpetually cranky spirit is said to pace the line where his fence once stood, shaking his preternatural fist and shouting, "You old black crows!"

These days, cafeteria workers working alone at night in the

Commons say they have been chased through the dining area by pushcarts moving on their own. Pots, pans, kitchen utensils, and food items have been thrown onto the floor by unseen hands.

Since 1901 the University of Portland has devoted itself to an education of the heart and mind by focusing on three central elements: teaching, faith, and service. Today the University is ranked among the top 10 schools in the West by U.S. News and World Report and is Oregon's major Catholic university, affiliated with the Congregation of Holy Cross.

UNIVERSITY OF PORTLAND
WILLIAMETTE BOULEVARD

# San Francisco, California

The Spanish founded the mission of "San Francisco de Asis" in June 1776. San Francisco became part of America in 1848 at the end of the Mexican-American War. San Francisco experienced rapid growth with the discovery of gold at nearby Sutter's Mill, and the ensuing 1849 California Gold Rush.

One of the defining events in San Francisco history is the 1906 Earthquake, when much of the city was leveled. But, San Francisco was able to recover fairly quickly.

## The Golden Gate Bridge Connects The Living and The Dead

Tourists in San Francisco can see sea lions, sample delicious local seafood, take the ferry to Alcatraz Island, and then travel under the Golden Gate Bridge. They'll hear all about the ghosts galore that haunt the nation's most notorious prison, but what may come as a surprise is to learn about the number of folk who jump from the Golden Gate Bridge ending their own lives.

The drop at low tide from the bridge is 222 feet, about the same distance as a twenty-story building. So, it's no surprise that, with an average of more than twenty suicides a year, the Golden Gate Bridge is one of the most haunted places in San Francisco.

Since it opened in 1937, the 4,200-foot Golden Gate Bridge has connected San Francisco and Marin County. Beyond the ghosts of jumpers, the crews of numerous boats and ships that have capsized here also haunt the bridge. Some of the ghosts appear on their phantom ships.

Take the missing steamer, the SS Tennessee, which is known to be a cause for much of the haunting around the Golden Gate Bridge. It disappeared in 1853 in the dense fog of Golden Gate Strait. Running afoul of the Gate's notorious current and rocks, she sank quickly only to rise again as a phantom. The phantom ship has been sighted by various credible witnesses over the years, often seen passing underneath the bridge, with its deck unmanned, only to fade into the fog minutes later.

Dozens of other ships have run aground or sunk in the straight. In 1901, the steamer SS City of Rio de Janeiro hit a rock; as the ship was listing, passengers fought for the limited seats in the lifeboats, but they ended up sinking them. Fistfights broke out over life jackets. In less than 18 minutes, 129 people were dead. Shaken survivors clung to debris and struggled to shore. The Golden Gate's cold waters have swallowed many sailors and suicides. On foggy nights, with the wind howling through the cables, one can hear the ghastly cries of men plummeting to their deaths.

THE GOLDEN GATE BRIDGE
SAN FRANCISCO BAY

## Ship of Ghosts Haunts San Francisco Bay

At San Francisco's Fisherman's Wharf, history, culture, and ethnic pride form a distinctive blend that gives it a strength and vitality all its own.

Indeed, anyone who has walked along the Embarcadero at this popular tourist spot is impressed and awed by the majestic ships that punctuate the renovated warehouses along the walkway.

From the Gold Rush days until the early 1900s, the city's fishing fleet was largely composed of lateen-rigged sailboats known as feluccas, very similar to the crafts the Italian fisherman used in their native land. Feluccas were ideal vessels for the rough waters around San Francisco, and the Italian immigrants were skillful and successful at the seafood trade. Today, the grandsons and great-grandsons of these past generations operate the fishing fleet and many of the Wharf's internationally acclaimed restaurants.

But, more than any other ship, The Balclutha, known as "The Ghost Ship of San Francisco Bay," is a site to behold and one that bewitches. The 1886 windjammer, a three-masted, square-rigged schooner, is permanently anchored at Hyde Street Pier for tourists and seafaring admirers to enjoy.

But, on many evenings, police are barraged by calls that the ship is seen sailing through the fog of San Francisco Bay. All too frequent calls to 911 proclaim: "the Balclutha has broken free and is drifting away."

When the police go to check on the Balclutha, there it is, anchored as usual. Instead, it was a ghost ship sailing the bay. It wasn't just any ship—it was an old-fashioned sailing ship, the kind with two masts and lots of rigging. Just like the Balclutha.

BALCLUTHA
HYDE AND JEFFERSON STREETS
SAN FRANCISCO MARITIME PARK

## Battle of The Sexes: Gender Struggle Continues to Haunt at San Francisco Mansion

It sounds like a fairy tale. Faxon D. Atherton, a poor adventurer from Massachusetts travels to Valparaiso, Chile in 1834 to become a trader in hides, tallow, foodstuffs, and other commodities.

By the 1860s, he'd built an extremely prosperous business and moves to California to make his family home. He brought along his bride – Dominga de Goni, daughter of a prominent Chileno family. The couple had seven children and lived in an estate in San Mateo County, which he called Valparaiso Park. Today, it's known as its own town: Atherton.

The glitch in the fairy tale was that Atherton was a notorious womanizer and traveled often. This alienated his wife and family.

After Atherton's death, Dominga moved into the city, San

Francisco. She built the Atherton Mansion on the corner of Octavia and California streets in the exclusive Pacific Heights district in 1881. Dominga lived there with her son George and his strong-willed wife, Gertrude. The two strong-willed women tortured poor George, constantly calling him "the weaker sex" and calling his manhood into question.

In 1887, in an attempt to get away from his feminine oppressors, George accepted an invitation to visit friends in Chile. After only a few days at sea, he died of kidney failure. His body was preserved in a barrel of rum and transferred to another ship back to San Francisco; when George's body was delivered, it was pickled in rum.

After George's death, both Dominga and Gertrude reported being awakened at night by knocks at their bedroom doors and by a cold and disturbing presence. The spirit of George apparently had decided to avenge itself on the women who'd tormented him in life. The phenomenon grew so troublesome that Dominga and Gertrude moved out.

But, the hauntings continued—the next several tenants moved out, one after another, saying the place was haunted. They said that they heard phantom knockings, felt cold spots, and saw the ghost of George, who was not a happy ghost.

In 1923, Dominga sold the property to an eccentric woman, Carrie Rousseau. She lived exclusively in the house's ballroom surrounded by more than fifty cats until her death in 1974. She rarely ventured into the other rooms.

After Rousseau's death, female ghosts, thought to be Dominga and Gertrude, also started to appear, as if they were continuing the ongoing battle of the sexes with George.

Since Carrie Rousseau's death, the mansion has been remodeled and made into several apartments. However, the manifestations still occur. Residents report moving cold spots, wind blowing through closed rooms, voices in the night, and knocking sounds.

A few years ago, a séance conducted by a psychic identified four separate spirits active in the house. Three were female spirits "who just don't like men," and one "frail" male spirit. The psychic believes the Atherton home is still haunted by the ghosts of Dominga, Gertrude, George, and now, Carrie Rousseau.

ATHERTON MANSION
1990 CALIFORNIA STREET

## Ghostly Cellblocks and Chilly Encounters

It is considered the most famous of America's prisons. Its movie credits give testimony to its popularity. The list includes The Rock, Birdman of Alcatraz, Dead Man Walking, Murder in the First, to name a few.

Today, Alcatraz is a popular tourist attraction and national park in the San Francisco Bay, with more than 1 million visitors each year. In the nineteenth century, it was an army fort; it began holding prisoners during the Civil War in 1861. Then, during the 1900s, civilian prisoners were sent there; by 1934, it was a federal prison. There, some of society's most hardened prisoners were sent, as it was considered inescapable. The guest roster included Robert "the Birdman" Stroud, George "Machine Gun" Kelly, and Chicago crime boss Al

Capone. The prison was the site of many murders, suicides, and beatings, and also a place where many inmates died or were killed trying to escape. Alcatraz was finally closed in May of 1963.

But its legacy remains strong, and its ghosts continue to haunt the thousands of visitors each day who take a ferry from Fisherman's Wharf across the bay to get a firsthand glimpse of this infamous institution. Guards and tour guides report hearing sounds of cells being opened and closed, footsteps, whistling, screams, and voices echoing down the halls. Visitors have heard moans, agonized cries, and chains rattling in cell blocks B and C.

The D cellblock, where prisoners were held in solitary confinement, and where visitors can enter the spooky cellblocks, is haunted as well. Most visitors report feeling a really creepy feeling in this wing of the prison, one that sends chills up their spines. Confinement in the D cellblock was particularly harrowing and those who disobeyed would be sent there for seven days with only one brief ten-minute shower during that time.

Many Rangers and Park Service staff have recounted stories of cell doors mysteriously closing and opening, unexplainable sounds and loud noises, a feeling of being watched, and a sense of terrible pain and suffering. Many psychic investigators and ghost hunters have picked up on the enormous amount of energy surrounding the prison and in the walls and cells, on the hard rock that was Alcatraz.

ALCATRAZ ISLAND
GOLDEN GATE RECREATIONAL AREA

## An Officer and a Gentle Ghost

From a fur trader's home to officers' quarters, the Haskell House in San Francisco's Fort Mason area has a colorful and rich history. And, this home of Leonides Haskell, an 1850s fur trader and abolitionist, developed a reputation of being haunted.

Built in 1851, the U.S. government took over the building in 1863. The government transformed it into quarters for its officers stationed at the San Francisco military base. It is reported that Fort Mason military personnel knew the two-story white frame house at the end of Franklin Street in the Presidio as Quarters Three.

The haunting is said to go back to the time when Haskell House was a private residence. In September 1857, when U.S. Senator David Broderick was visiting his friend and fellow abolitionist Haskell, he was killed in a gun duel with former Judge David Terry. The two disagreed strongly over slavery; Broderick was against it, Terry for it, and the two got into a dispute that ended tragically.

The argument became heated, and they decided to settle it with a duel. When the two men faced each other, Broderick's gun went off as he drew it from his holster. Terry fired back, striking the senator in the chest. Three days later, Broderick died at the Haskell home. The senator had spent the night before the duel at Haskell's house, where he paced about fretfully all night.

The house was later used by the Union Army as a residence for officers stationed at Fort Mason. Many of the officers who lived there over the years say that they had seen and heard Broderick's ghost pacing back and forth, apparently reliving his anguish the night before the confrontation. They say they feel his presence and have heard his pacing footsteps. Some have also heard taps at the window. An Army colonel who lived in the house reported, "I feel that something or someone follows me about the house at times. I even feel that it watches me in the shower."

Today, the site of the duel is a state landmark where the positions of each of the combatants are marked. The Haskell House is now part of the Golden Gate National Recreation Area and bears a sign testifying to its role as the site of the senator's death.

The location of Fort Mason itself makes this ghost haunting a popular tourist attraction. Located on the San Francisco waterfront between Fisherman's Wharf and the Golden Gate Bridge, Fort Mason Center offers people the opportunity to experience a unique urban recreational environment.

THE HASKELL HOUSE
GOLDEN GATE NATIONAL RECREATION AREA

## Benevolent Ghost Haunts Bell Tower

Some call them "Snob Hills." There is no question the affluent Nob Hill and Russian Hill areas of San Francisco draw swarms of tourists and are always abuzz with activity. But more hauntings are reported in this area than in any other section of San Francisco.

The old cemetery there, now buried under tons of concrete construction, is thought to be the source of the manifestations. And, at least a few of those lost souls seem to have found a home in the tower of the San Francisco Art Institute at 800 Chestnut Street, the building constructed next to the cemetery.

Built in 1926 on the north slope of Russian Hill, the San Francisco Art Institute rests upon grounds that once held the earthly remains of San Francisco's earliest residents. The monastic tower, which is adjacent to the cemetery site, has been considered haunted for many years.

Over the years, a variety of manifestations, including eerie flickering lights and power tools mysteriously turning on and off, have been reported by students and the public. At one point, the unexplained activity seemed to have ceased, and the harmless ghost was thought to have drifted away. That is, until the bell tower was being renovated as a storage area in 1968. Then, a series of near fatal accidents were blamed on the ghost, who was rearing his head again. Some construction workers were so frightened that they quit. A seance was held that year to get to the bottom of the mystery. It was confirmed that the lost graveyard and its souls were creating the havoc.

Other reports of sightings include one by a former student who was taking a break on the tower's third level when he heard footsteps coming up the stairs. He watched in disbelief as the door opened and closed, and the invisible footsteps went past him to the observation deck. Other students, a watchman, and a janitor have also encountered apparitions climbing the stairs of the tower. Some years later, students partying in a room at the top of the tower had a similar experience.

These days, the tower is closed. The school says it's unsafe, citing seismic concerns, but others believe it is for paranormal reasons. They think it is because the ghosts of the San Francisco Art Institute don't want people in their tower.

SAN FRANCISCO ART INSTITUTE
800 CHESTNUT STREET

## Sleepless in San Francisco

It may be called "The Queen Anne Hotel," but it is the spirit of a ghost named Mary who continues to provide the ambiance, or the creepy factor, for guests in this quaint century-old San Francisco mansion. Some call her the friendliest ghost in town. And others report there are times when she is not so nice. Interestingly, there are two schools of thought on Mary's personality, which leads some to speculate that she truly reveals both sides of her personality, the dark and the light.

Mary is thought to be the former headmistress for at a school she opened in 1890: Miss Mary Lake's School For Young Ladies. She makes herself known as a possessed and very frightening doll, a chair that knocks those who sit in it on the floor, and an elevator that leaves riders terrified.

Mary Lake once ran this finishing school for well-to-do San Francisco girls and ran it with a tight fist. She's been known to unpack visitor's luggage, and even tuck guests into bed. Sounds like nice gestures, but not for those hotel guests who are tired and ready for a good night's sleep who unexpectedly find this misty looking figure lurking over their beds. The most common reports are of unusual cold spots and seeing a misty figure in the shape of a woman.

The Mary sightings occur mostly on the fourth floor, where Mary was reported to have spent most of her time during her tenure at the school. In fact, room 410 used to be her office. It is no surprise, then, that visitors who happen to stay in room 410 may have very unusual experiences.

Walking down Sutter Street, on the edge of San Francisco's Pacific Heights, it is hard for anyone to miss the pink spectacle known as The Queen Anne Hotel. It had been constructed by Senator James Graham Fair for his two daughters, Theresa (Tessie) and Virginia (Birdie) Fair. Senator Fair, who went on to build the first Fairmont Hotel, was extremely wealthy from Nevada's famous Comstock Lode. He had been estranged from his two daughters, and he built the school in his hometown of San Francisco so that his daughters would be closer to him.

Located at 1590 Sutter Street, the building has changed hands numerous times since it closed down as a school in 1896. Now, it is a massive 50-room Victorian hotel that reigns over the Pacific Heights neighborhood from a prominent corner position. The Queen Anne Hotel, with its maroon interior walls, fringed lampshades, ornate carved chairs, plush dark red velvet curtains and antique/Victorian decorating is filled with atmosphere. Guests say they feel like they've stepped back into another era.

A spooky era, perhaps. One guest called his ghostly experience with Mary on the elevator "The Tower of Terror." For the rest of his stay, he took the stairs to his fourth floor room, refusing to undergo the bone-chilling grind of the hidden pulleys, the lights buzzing off and on in the vintage elevator, and the feeling he was not alone.

Guests have taken photos during their stay at the Queen Anne, and they often include orbs in the background. In the lobby, there is an old-fashioned Victorian doll that some say opens and closes its eyes and makes faces at them. Some believe that the doll now houses Miss Mary's spirit.

QUEEN ANNE HOTEL
1590 SUTTER STREET

## The Ghost Next Door: Pacific Heights Called the Bermuda Triangle of Spiritualist churches

San Francisco's exclusive Pacific Heights is a tree-lined neighborhood dotted with spectacular Victorian homes that overlook a panoramic view of the Marina and the Golden Gate Bridge. It is home to the rich, the famous, and a group of personalities who literally are out of this world.

Local ghost hunters say the ghost stories are steeped in the area's rich history and that there is high supernatural activity partially because of the large number of Spiritualist churches in the area. Not to mention the much-haunted Alcatraz Island, which is easily spotted from this perch view.

Like the Who's Who of Pacific Heights residents, the ghosts also have established monikers. There's Mary Ellen Pleasant, the mother of civil rights in California and feared voodoo queen of San Francisco, Mary Lake who resides in a spirit sense at the Queen Anne Hotel, and Flora Summerton, the ghost of California Street. Atop the hills of Pacific Heights, an innocent young woman rides an evening cable car, stalked by her handsome fiancé.

PACIFIC HEIGHTS, SAN FRANCISCO

## Mr. Whittier Is Home

What better tourist attraction than a ghost. And that's what visitors to the California Historical Society used to find when they stop in for a tour. Today, the mansion is a private residence.

The Society's home is perched on the side of a hill that once was the mansion of William Franklin Whittier, head of what would become known as the Pacific Gas and Electric Company. Built in 1896, the 16,000 sq. ft., four story, 30-room mansion was unusual for its day because it was built of brick, wood, and red sandstone.

The mansion survived the 1906 earthquake and was sold when Whittier died at the age of 85 in 1917. It became San Francisco's German Consulate. In the post-war years it was used by the Philosophical Institute until 1956, when it became home to the historical society. During the years the mansion was home to the historical society, and tours were a daily occurrence, many unexplained occurrences took place in the mansion, mostly centered around the basement and servant quarters, where visitors report seeing shadowy outlines and feeling ice cold spots. Many said they didn't actually see anyone, but they had a strong feeling they were not alone.

Some believe the ghost to be that of Mr. Whittier. Others say the ghost is Whittier's son, Billy. Billy was a wild and crazy guy who lived for wine, women, and song. He is said to haunt the wine cellar.

WHITTIER MANSION
2090 JACKSON STREET
PRIVATE RESIDENCE

## The Hostess with the Mostest

She's been called the "Mother of Civil Rights" for the work that Mary Ellen Pleasant began in the 1860s. She was born into slavery, and her mother brought her up in the Voodoo religion. Mary Ellen herself was perceived to have priestess powers. Whether she had supernatural powers or not, she certainly amassed a fortune in San Francisco; she was reportedly worth $30 million at its peak.

There is now a park and memorial plaque at the corner of Bush and Octavia streets, where her grand mansion once stood. She was hostess to the most wealthy and influential people of the town at her home, and it was said that Mary used hidden peepholes and passages to spy on her guests' conversations while she was out of the room. Her Voodoo prowess legend lives on to this day, as does the belief that she haunts the park where her house once stood. If anyone disses her name, she, or her ghost, gets mad, and objects suddenly get thrown at them or fall on them. Some say she appears as a crow, thus is better able to drop objects.

MARY ELLEN PLEASANT
BUSH and OCTAVIA STREETS

## Special Service at The Hotel Majestic

Another survivor of the 1906 Earthquake, the Hotel Majestic, is said to be haunted by the ghost of the former owner.

As San Francisco's oldest continually operating hotel, it was once the private residence of Milton Schmidt, a turn-of-the-century railroad magnate and member of the California State Legislature. In 1904, after Senator Schmidt was not re-elected, it became a hotel. Though the hotel is said to be a refuge from the hustle-bustle of San Francisco, guests on the fourth floor say they are kept awake all night long by ghosts. In one room, the bathtub mysteriously fills itself with water. The ghost is reported to walk the hallways of the fourth floor at night, clanking his keys along the wall. Some guests report their beds being shaken. Many assume it is an earthquake, but it isn't.

HOTEL MAJESTIC
1500 SUTTER STREET

# San Jose, California

The Spanish founded San Jose in 1777 as a farming town. It grew greatly in size in the years after the Second World War. It is now the capital of Silicon Valley. And, it is home to a very unusual tourist attraction, which happens to be haunted.

## Do You Know the Way to San Jose: Stairways to Nowhere and a Maze of Mystery

It was tragedy that led Sarah Winchester to find the ghosts. Once a prominent member of elite Boston society, Sarah became distraught following the death of her only child, a daughter, and her husband, the heir to the Winchester rifle founders.

Legend has it that Sarah believed that fate took her husband and child because of the bad karma caused by the family business—the manufacture of rifles instrumental in killing people—which resulted in a curse over the Winchester family.

According to the story, Sarah believed the only way to appease the evil spirits was to build a monument to her dead family members and keep the construction going. It was important that the house never be completed. In 1884 at age 44, she traveled alone to San Jose, California, to build what would become the seven-story Winchester Mystery House.

It is a rambling, 160-room unfinished and unfurnished house. Construction would become an ongoing process for almost forty years. Now, there are four stories (it was changed after the 1906 earthquake), 1,257 windows, 10,000 windowpanes, 467 doorways, 47 fireplaces (gas, wood, and coal), forty bedrooms, five or six kitchens, forty staircases, 52 skylights, and two basements.

Curiosities include staircases leading to nowhere and doors in the floor. History reveals that Sarah Winchester started it all, as far as the ghost sightings are concerned. She was the first to report spirits in the hall, and she rang a bell at midnight to summon the ghostly spirits, and another at 2 a.m. to bid them goodnight.

In 1903, Theodore Roosevelt, who was then president, passed through San Jose and called at the Winchester Mansion. He was turned away with the message that "the house was not open to strangers." According to servants' tales, the only guests that Sarah entertained were spectral ones.

These days, the unusual goings-on reported in the Winchester House include organ music in the Blue Room where Sarah died, a couple lingering in the corner of a bedroom, cold spots in Sarah's bedroom, and apparitions of Sarah. Perhaps one of the oddest is the smell of chicken soup coming from a long-unused kitchen.

Since Sarah Winchester's death, several psychics have reported feeling cold spots and seeing red balls of light that fade and explode. Psychic Jeanne Borgen visited in 1975 and reportedly took on Sarah Winchester's appearance for a short time. Authors Richard Winer and

Nancy Osborn spent the night there in 1979 while researching a book and were awakened by footsteps and piano music.

Staff members have also reported seeing apparitions and lights going on and off, hearing whispering sounds, and security alarms being triggered from inside the house. Apparitions of Sarah have also been photographed.

These days the house is a tourist attraction and is open for visitors of all kinds.

THE WINCHESTER MYSTERY HOUSE
525 SOUTH WINCHESTER BLVD.

# Los Angeles, California

It's known as the City of Dreams, but in Los Angeles, the shadows of loss and unfulfilled dreams create a palpable presence, one that is almost haunting. And, in many cases, IS haunting.

Take Sunset Strip, the legendary evening hotspot where signs warn partygoers that there is no cruising. That, however, doesn't seem to scare off the ghosts that haunt many locales along the strip.

## Laugh In: Spooks Take Center Stage at L. A. Comedy Club

Think Hollywood. Think comedy. And, famous comedians like Steve Martin, Robin Williams, Jay Leno, Jim Carrey, and Roseanne pop into mind. This troupe of "Who's Who" on the comedy front all got their starts at the Comedy Store at 8433 Sunset Boulevard, West Hollywood.

But perhaps not as well known is the fact that sometimes these comics have had to share center stage at the popular Sunset Strip haunt with a ghostly cast of characters. These apparitions have been haunting the popular comedy club since it opened its doors in the same location as the 1940s most famous glamorous nightclub, Ciro's.

Some of the ghosts are thought to be mobsters, who hung out there in the early days and who continue to preside over the joint, with its three rooms/stages where comedy plays out seven nights a week.

Once a popular hangout of show biz people and gangsters back in the 1940s into the 50s, in the 1960s it was a rock club, featuring the Doors, the Byrds, and other L. A. bands. Later, it reopened as the Comedy Store, where it has been the launch pad for many of today's well-known comics.

The most popular, albeit least-liked, ghost is said to be the infamous gangster Mickey Cohen. During the days of yore, the mob "had its fingers in this club," and gangster Cohen was known to shake down the place at least once a week. He carried out unpleasant mob business in the basement of the place. According to the stories, the mob tough guy has returned to his old haunts; he was even known to heckle the late comedian Sam Kinison.

Another story is that one night comic Blake Clarke was locking up the club, pulling a metal grate across the basement entrance to padlock it, when something kept pushing at him from behind the door. The grate was pulled out of the wall, but then it snapped back into place. That's when a giant figure of a man stood before him making growling noises and continuing to move toward him. Clarke ran away and vowed never to return. Months later, the club's manager sent Clarke downstairs again. This time, he brought a friend, and they were approached again by the menacing shadow of a large man. They scooted out of there.

Luckily, the other ghosts at the Comedy Store are reported to be friendlier.

There are least four other ghosts that hang around the building, all that originate from the 1940s and 1950s. They become most active when the place is quiet, especially in the early morning hours.

In 1994, a segment for the TV series, "Haunted Hollywood," was filmed in the original main room. Ghost hunters who came along to watch the taping say they saw three men, all dressed in 1940s style suits, in the back of the room, but when they looked again, the images suddenly disappeared.

These days, patrons will get a glimpse of the rising comic stars of Hollywood. Other major stars who have appeared at the Comedy Store include Eddie Murphy, David Brenner, Jimmie Walker, Whoopi Goldberg, Louie Anderson, Byron Allen, Paul Rodriguez, and Garry Shandling.

The Comedy Store was opened by the parents of comedian Pauley Shore; his mother, Mitzi Shore, still owns it. In 2005, cable channel TBS ran an unscripted comedy series called "Minding the Store", starring Pauley Shore running the family business for his mother.

THE COMEDY STORE
8433 SUNSET BOULEVARD

## Global Nomads and Ghosts Make Chateau Marmont Most Glamorous Hotel in Hollywood

Although it is a glamorous refuge for the rich and famous, the beautiful hotel on the hill, the Chateau Marmont, holds its share of tragedy–and ghosts who haunt to tell.

A young William Holden was told: if stars want to get naughty, the Chateau Marmont was the place to do it. Located at 8221 Sunset Boulevard, the hotel is where Clark Gable and Jean Harlow started their affair while she was on her honeymoon with another man. It's the place where Howard Hughes was a frequent guest in the penthouse; he was known to spy on the girls around the pool with his binoculars. Sadly, it is also the hotel where John Belushi overdosed.

The 1929, eighteenth-century chateau-style building is quintessential Hollywood with its fluted pillars and ivy. The lobby lends its own spooky motif, with its gothic vaulted ceilings and dark wood. It has played hosts to numerous celebrities over the years, including John Lennon, Clark Gable, Marilyn Monroe, Jean Harlow, Dustin Hoffman, Greta Garbo, and dozens of others who wanted to be alone, or were just looking for a little privacy.

Some of the famous Chateau Marmont stories include Jim Morrison of the Doors hurting his back here while dangling from a drainpipe, trying to swing from the roof into the window of his hotel room. Read-throughs were held at the hotel for "Rebel Without a Cause;" James Dean and Natalie Wood met here for the first time. When actor Montgomery Clift was almost killed in a 1956 auto accident, Elizabeth Taylor brought him to the Chateau Marmont, where she leased the penthouse as a place for him to recuperate.

It is also said to be haunted by a number of ghostly spirits. And, this being the Marmont, one has even been known to climb into guest's beds.

THE CHATEAU MARMONT
8221 SUNSET BOULEVARD

## L.A. Story: Hollywood Sign Shines Spotlight on Lost Souls

Despite, or maybe because of, the glitter and glamour of Hollywood, many of the ghosts that haunt Tinsel Town are sad ghosts, lost souls who represent wanna-be stars and starlets who felt they were Hollywood failures.

The world-famous Hollywood sign is an L.A, landmark, and the site of one of the saddest ghost stories. The sign, which is perched on Mount Lee in Griffith Park, looming over Los Angeles, is rumored to be haunted by the spirit of a distraught actress who leapt to her death from one of the larger-than-life letters.

Her name was Lillian Millicent "Peg" Entwhistle, and local press proclaimed at the time of her death that she set a new standard for suicide in Hollywood. Her suicide—jumping off the letter "H" on the Hollywoodland sign, brought her a notoriety she never experienced in life. And, it's said that her spirit, which continues to haunt the popular tourist attraction, has brought her further fame among Hollywood ghost hunters and those who experience her presence today.

The original sign—with its 30-foot-wide and 50-foot-high letters—was built in 1923 to encourage the sales of homes in the Hollywoodland subdivision, which was located along Beachwood Canyon. Like everything else in Tinsel Town, the sign was never meant to last. Studded with low wattage light bulbs, and a frequent target of vandals, the sign eventually fell into complete disrepair by the late 1930s.

Finally in 1949, the Hollywood Chamber of Commerce repaired and rebuilt the sign. They also removed "land" from the line of letters so that it merely read "Hollywood." But, it continued to deteriorate, until the late 1970's, when a fund-raising campaign was begun to replace the letters. Donors were asked to contribute $27,700 each to buy a replacement letter. In 1978, the original sign was replaced with new all-steel letters. The sign now stretches 450 feet along the side of Mount Lee and remains 50 feet tall. Today, it stands as a definitive symbol of Hollywood and the film industry.

Only 24-years-old at the time of her tragic death, "Peg" made her acting debut in New York at 17. While working on Broadway, Peg met a fellow actor named Robert Keith, who was a popular star; the two soon fell in love and got married. But the marriage soured quickly. During a visit to her mother-in-law's house, Peg noticed a photograph of a young boy on the mantel. She asked who he was and was informed that he was Robert's son from his first marriage, something that he had kept hidden from her. Incidentally, that surprise stepson was future actor Brian Keith, star of the television show "Family Affair."

For various reasons, the marriage ended, and they were soon divorced.

Meanwhile, The Great Depression had arrived, and Peg's career was not going well. She moved to Hollywood, where she found work in small film parts and the theater, but not too much work. Fame was fleeting, and then in her early twenties, she was just another pretty face in a sea of Hollywood wannabes.

On a September night in 1932, she told friends and relatives she was going out for a walk, and was found dead a few days later at the foot of the Hollywood sign. Sadly, just after her death, her relatives received a letter that she had won the lead role in a Beverly Hills Playhouse production. Ironically, the part was a beautiful young woman who commits suicide in the final act of the play.

For decades and still today, hikers, tourists and park rangers in Griffith Park have reported seeing a woman dressed in 1930s era clothing who abruptly vanishes when they approach her. Her description is exactly Peg, a pretty young blonde who seems very sad. Others report being overwhelmed by the heavy smell of a gardenia perfume, which was known to be Peg's trademark.

Eyewitnesses who spot Peg say she seems very sullen, walking around almost in a daze. Usually she only appears very late at night, especially when it is very foggy. And, rangers say her presence often triggers the sign's alarm system. When police and park rangers go to investigate, no one is there. Motion detectors will state otherwise, showing someone standing within five feet of the sign.

THE HOLLYWOOD SIGN
MT. LEE, HOLLYWOOD, CALIFORNIA
(Please note: the sign is closed off and is not accessible to the public.)

## At the Movies: Fame Isn't Fleeting for the Stage 28 Ghost

On any given day, visitors to Universal Studios Amusement Park in Hollywood might bump into the filming of the popular TV show "Desperate Housewives," feel like they are on fire when they enter the "Backdraft " studio, or get drenched on the roller coaster ride in "Jurassic Park," not to mention getting goose bumps from the Bates Motel and the setting of Alfred Hitchcock's classic thriller "Psycho."

Almost from the beginning, Universal opened their studios to the public for tours, but they have since added theme park rides. You can not only see real shows and movies being made, but go on scary rides.

But, in this mega-amusement park, home to where many of the top horror films and ghost stories were filmed, there're spooky stories that may inspire fear in some who tour the amusement park: the ghost of Stage 28.

Lon Chaney was one of horror's greatest stars, who now appears as a caped figure haunting Stage 28. Many studio employees and visitors who don't know the history of Stage 28 have reported seeing a man in a black cape. He is often seen running on the catwalks overhead. Even security guards who laughed off the idea of a resident ghost, admit to being "spooked" by lights that turn on and off by themselves and by doors that open and close on the empty stage at night.

But, Universal isn't the only Hollywood studio that is haunted. Down the road at Paramount Studios the spirit of Rudolph Valentino spooks visitors. The Sheik's shimmering specter has been seen floating among old garments in the costume department.

UNIVERSAL STUDIOS
UNIVERSAL STUDIOS BLVD.
Off 101 Hollywood Freeway North

## Pet Story: Phantom Pets of Filmdom

Many Hollywood stars have lived on forever as ghosts. But stars are not the only ones whose fame doesn't stay buried. Many stars of the big screen and television have buried their beloved animal companions at the Los Angeles Pet Memorial Park.

Tucked away in the lush green rolling hills of Calabasas, California, the ten landscaped acres of the Los Angeles Pet Memorial Park provide a serene and peaceful resting place for more than 40,000 animal companions.

There lies Punkie Barrymore, cat of Lionel Barrymore, a childhood pet of Lauren Bacall's, and Morey Amsterdam's dog, named Pussy Cat. Adam Sandler 's beloved pit bull, Meatball, is buried there as well as Hopalong Cassidy's horse, Mary Pickford's dog, and Petey, The Little Rascals' dog.

And, some of the animal spirits are not resting, as visitors report frequent canine and feline ghostly happenings. Several visitors to the dog cemetery report being licked by a phantom dog, or have heard panting and barking sounds.

The spirit of Rudolph Valentino's Great Dane, Kabar, is active and barking here—it may be the ghost that gets the most attention. The dog died in 1929 but has since returned as a ghost.

Like just about everything in LA, this is no ordinary dog cemetery. The park's Rainbow Garden, located near the front entrance, affords guests an opportunity for reflection in a calm, picturesque setting. One historical feature of note is the brick mausoleum, which was erected in 1929, and is the oldest original structure on the property.

Granite markers bear inscriptions in English, French, Spanish, Hebrew, Russian, Italian, and many other languages. Symbols of various religious faiths are also widely represented. Some markers bear images of beloved pets embossed on the stone. Flowers, photographs, and ornaments adorn numerous burial sites.

The park was founded and dedicated on September 4, 1928. It is, therefore, one of the oldest facilities of its kind on the West Coast. Recognizing the need for decent and dignified pet burials, the Rollins and Dr. Eugene Jones family owned and operated the facility for more than forty years. In 1973, the family graciously donated the cemetery to the Los Angeles. After managing the park for a decade, the city considered selling the property to developers.

A small group of pet owners learned of this and established S.O.P.H.I.E., Inc. ("Save Our Pets' History in Eternity"), a nonprofit public benefit corporation dedicated to the preservation of this beautiful sanctuary. S.O.P.H.I.E. members initiated a fundraising drive to purchase the grounds and lobbied at the state legislature in Sacramento to enact the first-ever state law to protect pet cemeteries. On September 12, 1986, S.O.P.H.I.E. dedicated the Los Angeles Pet Memorial Park in perpetuity.

LOS ANGELES PET MEMORIAL PARK
5068 NORTH OLD SCANDIA LANE

# San Diego, California

The first European to visit the region was explorer Juan Rodriguez Cabrillo in 1542. The name of San Diego was given to the area in 1602. In 1769, a Spanish military post, the Presidio of San Diego, was established. Around the same time, Franciscan friars founded the Mission San Diego de Alcala. Today, San Diego is the second-largest city in California, and the seventh-largest city in the United States.

## Beautiful Stranger: The Ghost of Kate Morgan and the Hotel Del Coronado

The afternoon sun washes over the grassy expanse of the Windsor Lawn, across a terrace of tables and in through the open doors of the Spa & Fitness Center at the luxurious Hotel del Coronado in the San Diego Bay. Then, suddenly, lights start flickering, doors slam—as if being pushed by an invisible force. A massage therapist in the middle of a client's herbal wrap struggles to open up a treatment table that just won't budge. Facials stop. Massages halt. Manicures melt. Exfoliations end. "Looks like Kate's back," says Meg Kruse, manager of the spa. "Whenever weird things start happening, we know someone is about to see her."

Forget that ten American presidents bedded down beneath the signature red-turreted roof. Or, that the Hotel Del was the backdrop for the cinematic frolic of Jack Lemmon and Tony Curtis and the glamorous and cavorting Marilyn Monroe in Some Like It Hot. Or that it was also the inspiration and influence for The Wizard of Oz author L. Frank Baum.

It was Kate Morgan who captured and continues to inspire major headlines as the ghost who has made herself quite comfortable, and fairly active, within the walls of this nineteenth-century hotel, the crowning point of the Coronado, California, peninsula. She, and her aura, has spun a richly layered history since the day the then 24-year-old wife and beauty checked into the Hotel Del on Thursday, November 24, 1892.

One-third sun. One-third sand. One-third fairy tale. A classic historic hotel, this seaside resort was built in 1888, and designated a National Historic Landmark in 1977. Art, architecture, film, and history buffs point to the Hotel Del Coronado as one of the most prominent and historic places in the country to hang your hat.

A beautiful place to spend a few days lapping up luxury, the Hotel Del has been described as part fairy-tale castle, part luxury steamship. Rich features include the Babcock & Story Bar, home to the hotel's original 46-foot, hand-carved mahogany bar that was shipped around Cape Horn in 1888, with a view of the oceanfront through palms and French doors. The Hotel also boasts a host of modern-day amenities including the revamped oceanfront spa and fitness center and proximity to the main boulevard in Coronado, Orange Avenue, which was designed to guide visitors through a picturesque downtown and deposit them at the Del's front door.

In 1885, when Midwestern businessmen Elisha Babcock and Hampton Story bought the entire uninhabited Coronado peninsula for $110,000, it was predicted that the oceanfront property would become the talk of the western world.

Despite the ambiance and smorgasbord of activities from surfing and kayaking to poolside lounging and croquet, the ghostly goings-on also continue to attract attention among visitors at Hotel Del. With guests requesting Kate Morgan's room and keeping it booked year-round, hotel owners have talked about adding other activities around her aura—sleepovers in the room for teens, storytelling sessions, and so on.

No question, many of the Hotel Del guests want to know the Kate Morgan story.

Five days after Kate registered under the alias of Lottie A. Bernard from Detroit, she was found dead on a hotel exterior staircase. Because little was known about her identity, the press referred to this mysterious woman who spent five days at the Del as "the Beautiful Stranger."

Today the mystery and questions remain. Who was this beautiful stranger? According to police reports, Kate had a gunshot wound to the head, and it was assumed she had taken her own life. But no one has ever been completely sure that is true. Others argue that her husband, Tom, murdered her.

Guests and employees alike have tried to answer the question: "Why does Kate Morgan's spirit remain at the Del?" Some think she is still waiting for her husband Tom to join her. Others believe that without family and a permanent home, she has nowhere else to go. Still others believe Kate Morgan doesn't want to leave the Del because she likes "living" there, says Hotel Del historian Christine Donahue.

According to the Kate legend, Tom and Kate Morgan were a married couple who rode the trains in the late 1800s. Their occupation: con artists. Kate was apparently very attractive, and would lure men into a game of cards with her "brother" (Tom), so that they could prove their worth. Tom would swindle them out of whatever money they were willing to part with, and this is how the Morgans made their living.

In November of 1892, however, Kate discovered she was pregnant and wanted to stop the train racket and settle down. While the two were riding towards San Diego, they had an argument because Tom did not want to change his lifestyle. Tom disembarked at either Los Angeles or Orange County. He was supposed to meet Kate in San Diego for Thanksgiving.

Kate continued on to San Diego and checked into the Hotel Del Coronado under the name "Lottie Anderson Bernard." There she waited for Tom, but Thanksgiving came and went with no sign of him. During this time, Kate complained to various staff members of feeling ill and reports of the time indicate that she was looking especially pale. It is suspected that she may have performed an abortion on herself.

It is known that while Kate was waiting for her missing husband, she ventured into the city and bought a gun. It was shortly after this that Kate was found shot in the head on some outside steps leading down to the beach, an apparent suicide.

Today, determined to experience the legend of Kate Morgan, guests book Room 3327, where Kate Morgan stayed, almost a year in advance, says Lauren Ash Donoho, director of public relations for the Hotel Del. The most common incidents they find are strange breezes, ghostly noises, and the pale figure of a young lady walking in a black lace dress. One time, a group of parapsychologists took more than thirty-seven abnormal readings in a single day. Guests in the room Kate stayed in have experienced oppressive feelings and have seen curtains moving even though the windows are closed. Other people swear they have heard murmurings coming from somewhere in the room. Kate's ghost has also been seen walking down hallways of the hotel and standing at windows.

An electrician has said that the light over the steps where Kate died will not stay lit. The bulb is replaced constantly, but the light always winks out. A guest also claims that while he was staying in one of the haunted rooms, he saw a face on the television (which was turned off at the time).Two hotel employees verified this sighting.

"A lot of guests who come in here for massages or spa treatments, are by nature sensitive to the psychic," says Hotel Del spa manager Kruse. "And, they all say there is an incredible phenomenon going on here. They say they have felt or seen Kate and know she is here. I don't believe or disbelieve, but I know there is a lot of psychic action going on here. And, the guests tell me they've seen or felt Kate."

HOTEL DEL CORONADO
1500 ORANGE AVENUE
(800) 468-3533 or (619) 435-6611

## Fandango Anyone? Ghosts Serve Up Good Times at San Diego Eatery

In Spanish, a fandango is a fast dance done in triple time. At The El Fandango Restaurant in San Diego, diners get the same vibe when whirling before their eyes—then disappearing—is the image of a woman decked out in Victorian attire, and not appearing particularly happy.

Yes, there is way more on the menu here than Mexican fare. A sad story comes to life through this ghost who is a reminder of the tragic fate of the building's original owners.

The El Fandango Restaurant, located in the Old Town Historical Park district, was built on the site of the Machado home that was destroyed by fire in 1858.

But it is the ghost of one of the Machado family members that still hangs around. Dressed in white, a woman is seen drifting or floating through the building, sometimes passing through walls and closed doors. Her expression has been reported as sad, or sometime angry. The lady in white never interacts with anyone who sees her, but just appears then vanishes.

She also likes to sit at a darkened corner table near one of the front windows, but only when the window shade is drawn shut, as she doesn't like the light. Many say she seems rather sad, though she never says a word. It's as if her spirit just lingers there, or as if she is searching for her family members. Indeed, they all met a very sad fate.

The patriarch of the Machado family, José Manuel Machado, was one of the first soldiers stationed at the Presidio of San Diego and one of the first settlers of Old Town. He was born in 1756 and arrived in San Diego in 1781. He married a young woman, Serafina Valdez, aged 20, when he was 53, in an arranged marriage, which produced fifteen children. Some of the children became important people in the history of San Diego. Some think that Serafina is the ghost.

Today, El Fandango is a two story, brownish cream-colored restaurant and a very popular San Diego spot. There is a banquet room upstairs, while downstairs there is a dining area, and two outside patios. The menu selections offered today reflect the rich mix of

Mexican and Continental cuisine, with French, English, Hawaiian, Alaskan, and American influences.

The traditional huge, special parties called Fandangos, thrown by rich families to celebrate major family events, inspired the name of the restaurant. The whole town would be invited, and were fed on the host's patio traditional Mexican dishes and beef, while enjoying musical entertainment. Close friends of the family were fed inside.

EL FANDANGO RESTAURANT
2734 CALHOUN STREET

## Card Shark Deals Some Spooky Goings-on at Horton Grand Hotel

It is no surprise that when visitors stay at the elegant Horton Grand Hotel, which has been rebuilt brick-by-brick on the exact site of Ida Bailey's original 1880 - 1912 "cat house," some spooky surprises await them. The present location was at the heart of the infamous Gas Lamp (historical red-light) District, which is now part of a major downtown renovation. During the wild booming days of San Diego's rapid growth period, this part of town was the place for the saloons, brothels, opium dens, gambling halls, and brothels—with a few legitimate businesses mixed in.

San Diego was such a wide-open town that, at the time of a

police raid on November 11, 1912, the Mayor of San Diego and three Councilmen were picked up by the police while visiting Ida Bailey's brothel. The politicians had gotten the dates mixed up, and forgot to stay away that night.

The Horton Grand Hotel was scheduled for demolition in the 1970s, but instead it was dismantled and rebuilt in its present location. During the restoration, the 100-year-old grand oak staircase from The Grand Horton Hotel was carefully taken apart and sent to Austria where it was carefully repaired and restored to the glorious state it is now. The Grand Horton Hotel reopened in its new location in 1986.

Described as being an "elegant, ornate" Victorian structure, it was modeled after the Innsbruck Inn in Austria. But it was also smack dab in the red-light district, where it too was home to gambling and was once a brothel.

Today, the spirit of those times leaves on in a haunting way.

Meet Roger Whitaker—the number one ghost guest, who haunts the hotel, especially room 309. It seems that Roger was a gambler (card player) down on his luck. In a failed attempt to cover mounting gambling debts, Roger was caught one night cheating in a game of cards. Barely escaping with his life, he tried to hide in an armoire in his hotel room, number 309, but was soon found and shot to death by an angry gunman. Now, the spirit of Roger Whitaker still haunts Room 309 and the hallway outside the room.

Roger Whitaker has made numerous appearances. One guest saw him in the hallway, and he looked so real, she asked him where the ice machine was located. Imagine her surprise when he disappeared before her eyes.

Room 309 guests have been awakened in the middle of the night by the bed being shaken and the armoire's doors being opened. Lights have been known to have a will of their own, turning on and off. Objects in the room have been known to move by themselves. The temperature in the room can become unexplainably warm, unaffected by the air conditioning or opening a window. At other times, the room becomes very cold. People in the hall have heard sounds of someone playing cards, even when the room is locked and vacant.

Several other ghosts are known to graciously haunt the Horton Grand and join Roger. Fortunately, they are all very polite at the Horton Grand.

One is rumored to be the aforementioned Madam Ida Bailey. As a former brothel owner and businesswoman, she was, among most things, always very hospitable. Some think it is her spirit that makes visitors welcome.

Other ghosts, thought to be from those earlier times, flock to the grand staircase. One evening, a visitor witnessed a group of spirits dressed in formal 1880s attire floating down the staircase together.

HORTON GRAND HOTEL
311 ISLAND AVENUE

## The Most Haunted House in the United States

Located in historic Old Town San Diego, the Whaley House has earned the title of "the most haunted house in the U.S.," and is one of only two houses in the state of California certified as haunted.

Built in 1857 by Thomas Whaley on land that was once a cemetery, the house is home to dozens of ghosts.

Thomas Whaley was an extremely successful man in business and society, and one of San Diego's most prominent citizens; his house was for a time the center of San Diego society. The San Diego county courthouse even rented the first floor from Mr. Whaley for a time to use as a city courtroom. Whaley had six children, and Corinne Lillian Whaley, the youngest, lived in the house until her death at the age of 89 in 1953.

The demolition of the Whaley House was prevented in 1956 by the formation of the Historical Shrine Foundation of San Diego County, which bought the land and the building. Eventually San Diego County was convinced to preserve the house as a historical museum. Over time, the Whaley House was restored to its original splendor, as it remains to this day.

Today it is a museum, opened to the public in 1960.

Modern day visitors report apparitions, cold spots, feelings of being touched, unexplainable lights, footsteps, rappings, moving objects, and odd smells. The feeling of being watched is a common occurrence at the house since it was opened as a museum. Many people, from volunteers to guests, have observed the haunting and strange happenings.

Author DeTraci Regula shares her experience at The Whaley House: "Over the years, while dining across the street at the Old Town Mexican Café, I became accustomed to noticing the shutters of the second-story windows open while we ate dinner, long after the house was closed for the day. On one visit, I could feel the energy in several spots in the house, particularly in the courtroom where I also smelled the faint scent of a cigar, supposedly Mr. Whaley's calling card. "

Famed ghost hunter Hans Holzer and psychic Sybil Leek discovered several spirits at the Whaley house. The multitude of ghosts at the Whaley House all have distinctive personas.

Though he died in 1890, Thomas Whaley, builder of the house, is still known as the "Lord of the House." His ghost is one of the most frequent, wearing a frock coat and top hat, and followed by the smell of cigar smoke. Some people say the smell is so overpowering, they have to leave the house. And, he's often heard laughing, a baritone laughter that resounds throughout the house.

Thomas' wife Anna Whaley, a petite, pretty woman who had a love of music, is often seen materializing from a ball of light and floating as if dancing with soft piano music playing. Like her husband's cigar smoke, her perfume – a sweet flowery scent - often permeates the air.

Another popular Whaley House ghost is "Yankee Jim" Robinson. Before the house was built, Yankee Jim was hung on the property for stealing a boat. He was a tall man—so tall, in fact, that when he was hanged, the gallows were a little too short, leaving him to suffocate under the hangman's noose. He haunted the house even when the Whaleys still lived there; and, today, Yankee Jim continues to roam the halls of The Whaley House.

Thomas, Anna, and Yankee Jim are the most active ghosts in the house, but there are others, including the Whaley's dog, Dolly. This dog can be found running down the halls, brushing up against people's legs, and chasing a ghostly cat through the rose garden into the house. Phantom dog panting also has also been heard in the house.

But the most common ghostly event is footsteps. Today, loud footsteps are heard upstairs when guests are downstairs, or when guests are upstairs, they often hear the footsteps downstairs.

WHALEY HOUSE
2482 SAN DIEGO AVENUE

# Resources

**Special Thanks:**

Beth Vagle-Freelance Researcher and Writer

Baltimore's Fell's Point Ghost Tours: Co-owners, Amy Lynwander and Melissa Rowell
**www.fellspointghost.com**

Charleston's Sandlapper Tours: Owner, Brian Collins
**www.sandlapperstours.com**

Charleston's Sandlapper Tour Guide and Co-Author, Ed Macy, co-author with Geordie Buxton, of two books on Charleston, *Haunted Charleston* and *Haunted Harbor*

Denver's The Brown Palace Hotel: Julia Kanellos, Historian and Archivists
**www.brownpalace.com**

Denver's Molly Brown House Museum: Kerri Atter, Director/Curator
**www.mollybrownhousemuseum.com**

Denver's The Oxford Hotel: Kathy Byrne, Sales and Marketing Director
**www.theoxfordhotel,com**

Louisville's Ghost Hunters Society: Keith Age, President
**www.louisvilleghs.com**

New Orleans's The Castle Inn and The Creole Gardens Guesthouse Bed and Breakfast: Co-owner, Andrew Craig
**www.castleinnofneworleans.com**
**www.creolegardens.com**

St. Augustine's The Ancient City Tours: Candace B. Fleming
**www.ancientcitytours.net**

San Diego's The Hotel Del Coronado: Meg Kruse, Spa Director and Lauren Ash Domoho, Director of Public Relations
**www.hoteldel.com**

Seattle's Haunted Happenings Seattle Ghost Tours: Owner, Jake
**www.privateeyetours.com**

# Ghost Tours

**General Tours:**
**www.historictours.com**
**www.hauntedamericatours.com**

**Albuquerque:**
New Mexico Ghost Tours
**www.nmghosttours.com**

**Atlanta:**
Atlanta does not have a Ghost Tour, but it does have a good history tour:
Guided History Tour
Underground Atlanta
404.523.2311 ext. 7025
**www.underground-atlanta.com**

**Baltimore:**
Fell's Point Ghost Tours
Co-Owners-Amy Lynwander & Melissa Rowell
**www.fellspointghost.com**
One of Baltimore's best ghost tours
Tours run March-November

**Boston:**
The Boston Harbor Association (Harborwalks)
374 Congress Street
Suite 609
Boston, Ma.
02219
617.482.1722
**www.tbha.org**
**www.bostonharborwalk.com**
**www.ghostsandandgravestones.com**
**www.newenglandghosttours.com**

**Charleston:**
Charleston has many tour companies and many provide ghost tours but for an unusual experience, try The Haunted Harbor Tour hosted by Ed Macy. A 45-foot seaworthy catamaran goes out six nights a week at 7:00 PM for an hour and a half of haunting fun. See Charleston from a ghostly perspective on the water and feel the thrill of the cool breezes and dark waves.

Sandlapper Tours, Inc.
Haunted Harbor Tours
Charleston Maritime Center
PO Box 21540
Charleston, South Carolina
29413
843.849.8687
**www.sandlappertours.com**

**Chicago:**
Chicago Hauntings Ghost Tours:
This is a popular tour of the Windy City's most authentic haunted sites. This tour of historically haunted sites lasts about three hours and visits numerous sites throughout the city, including Death Alley, Hull House (the most haunted house in Chicago), the St. Valentine's Day Massacre Site and much more. Book Chicago Hauntings Tour by calling toll-free at **1.888.446.7859.**
**www.chicagohauntings.com**

Richard Crowe Ghosts Tours:
Richard Crowe, who bills himself as a "professional ghost hunter," spins out ghost stories, legends, and lore on the four-hour trip. Reservations are required for each tour; call 708.499.0300 or visit **www.ghost-tours.com**

**Dallas/Fort Worth:**
Paranormal Ghost Tours
**www.paranormalghosts.com**

Fort Worth Convention and Tourism Bureau
**www.fortworth.com**

**Denver:**
**www.hauntedcolorado.net**

**Houston:**
**www.highspiritstours.com**

**Las Vegas:**
Haunted Las Vegas 1.800.633.1777
Haunted Vegas Tours 1.800.591.NILE

**Los Angeles:**
The Classic Haunted Hollywood Tour of Tinsel Town's Dark Side, sure to send chills & thrills up & down your spine. Customizable and private tours of famous death and scandal sites where spirits still wait for closure. You'll see the homes and hotels where celebrity ghosts still roam. Visit the cemetery of the stars, or even go inside Hollywood's' most haunted hotel, The Hotel Roosevelt, for a chance to make contact with the other side. Check out:
**www.hollywoodtours.com**

**www.starlinetours.com**

Los Angeles Ghosts-Special Events Services (Southern California)
1.800.738.6339

**Louisville:**
Ghost Hunters Society
Ghost Walks of Downtown Louisville
**www.louisvilleghs.com**
502.604.7013

**Memphis:**
Tours available-contact
See Memphis
1.800.235.7311

**Minneapolis:**
**www.wabashstreetcaves.com**

**Nashville:**
Nashville Ghost Tours
1.888.844.3999
**www.nashvilleghosttours.com**

**New Orleans:**
**www.neworleansghosttours.com**
**www.hauntedhistorytours.com**
**www.neworleanstours.com**
**www.neworleanstours.net**

**New York City:**
**www.newyorktalkandwalk.com**
**www.nycwalks.com**

**Philadelphia:**
History and Mystery Tours of Philadelphia
**www.philahistorytours.com**

Ghosts Tours of Philadelphia
**www.ghosttours.com**

**Phoenix:**
**www.ghostsofphoenix.com**

**Portland:**
13th Door Haunted House Ghost Tours Sponsored Haunting Productions, LLC, the tours are dedicated to providing visitors to Portland, Oregon area with the greatest haunted attraction in the Northwest. Call for reservations and information: **503.730.4579**

**St. Augustine:**
The Ancient City Tours, Inc.
3 Aviles Street
St. Augustine, Florida
32084
Phone- 904-827-0807
**www.ancientcitytours.net**

**Salt Lake City:**
Paranormal Ghost Tours
**www.paranormalghost.com**

**San Antonio:**
"The Ghosts & Legends of San Antonio" offered by America by Foot.
"The Best Tours in America's History" leaves nightly at 7 and 9 from the Gazebo at Alamo Park. Reservations for the tour are required and may be made locally by calling 271-9600 or toll-free 1-800-707-1186. They also may be made online at **www.sanantonioghosts.com.**

Spirits of San Antonio Tour:
1.210.493.2454
**www.alamocityghosttours.com**

**San Diego:**
**Ghosts and Gravestones Tours**
**www.ghostsandgravestonestours.com**

**San Francisco:**
**www.sfghosthunt.com**
**www.hauntedhaight.com**

**Savannah:**
Savannah Ghosts & Walking Tours:
There are many tours and to pick the one that suits you go to
**www.savannah.worldweb.com**
**www.hauntingstour.com**
**www.theghostofsavannah.com**
**www.savanahghoststours.net**

**Seattle:**
Haunted Happenings Seattle Ghost Tours
206-365-3739
Reservations required
**www.privateeyetours.com**

Jake's tours cover a large area of Seattle, visiting various locations of supernatural occurrences both past and present.
She also offers two different Mystery & Murder Tours covering the darker side of Seattle.
Van tours last 2 ?-3 Hours
Enjoy!

**Washington, D.C.**
Capital Hauntings Walking Tour-202-484-1565
**www.washingtonwalks.com**
**www.scaryplace.com**
**www.dcghosts.com**

## Archives

Atlanta Journal-Constitution Archives
Chicago Tribune Archives
Eastland Disaster Historical Archives
Eastland Memorial Society Archives
Los Angeles Times Archives
State Library of Louisiana Archives
Maryland Historic Trust Archives
Utah Department of Community and Culture Archives
Washington D.C. Historic Trust Archives

## Books


Adams, Charles, J. III, New York City Ghost Stories, Exeter House Books, 2005 edition

Burtinshaw, Julie, Romantic Ghost Stories. Ghost House Press, 2003

Hauck, Dennis William, National Directory of Haunted Places, Penguin, 1994

Holzer, Hans, Great American Ghost Stories, Barnes & Noble, 1990

Holzer, Hans, The Ghost Hunter, Barnes & Noble, 2005

Macy, Ed and Buxton, Geordie, Haunted Harbor, Charleston's Maritime Ghosts and the Unexplained, History Press, 2005

Macy, Ed and Buxton, Geordie, Haunted Charleston, Stories from The College of Charleston, The Citadel and The Holy City, History Press, 2004

Nadler, Holly Mascott, Ghosts of Boston Town, Three Centuries of True Hauntings, Down East Books, 2002

Taylor, Troy, Field Guide to Haunted Graveyards, Whitechapel Production Press, 2003

Taylor, Troy, Haunted Chicago: History and Hauntings of the Windy City, Whitechapel Productions Press, 2003


## WebSites


www.about.com
www.aghost.us.com
www.allaboutghosts.com
www.alamocityghosttours.com
www.ancientcitytours.com
www.artsandmusicpa.com
www.askyewolfe.com
www.atlanta.citysearch.com
www.baltimorestories.com
www.bedandbreakfastofsavannah.com
www.bostonharborwalk.com
www.bostonisland.org
www.brownhotel.com
www.brownpalace.com
www.castleinnofneworleans.com
www.chicagohauntings.com
www.citypaper.com
www.creolegardens.com
www.dcghosts.com
www.dchauntings.com
www.egha.net
www.famousamericans.net
www.fellspointghost.com
www.florida.worldweb.com
www.forthworth.com
www.georgiamagazine.com
www.ghostsandgravestones.com
www.ghostmag.com
www.ghostofphoenix.com
www.ghosttours.com
www.ghosttraveller.com
www.hauntedamericatours.com
www.hauntedcolorado.net
www.hauntedhaight.com
www.hauntedhistorytours.com
www.hauntedhouses.com
www.hauntednevada.com
www.haunted-places.com
www.hauntingstour.com
www.highspiritstours.com
www.historicghost.com
www.historictours.com
www.historictrust.com
www.hoteladolphus.com
www.hoteldel.com
www.hollywoodtours.com

www.infonavigate.com
www.johnnorrisbrown.com
www.legendsofamerican.com
www.louisvilleghs.com
www.lvol.com
www.marylandghosts.com
www.mass.gov
www.memphis.cityserach.com
www.mhtbrooklyn.org
www.mnghsc.com
www.molyybrownhousemuseum.com
www.morrisjumel.org
www.mtsusidelines.com
www.nashville.about.com
www.nashvilleghosttours.com
www.newenglandcuriosities.com
www.newenglandghosttours.com
www.neworleansghostours.com
www.neworleanstours.com
www.neworleanstours.net
www.newyorktalkandwalk.com
www.nmghosttours.com
www.npa.gov
www.nycwalks.com
www.orpheum-memphis.com
www.paranormal.about.com
www.paranormalghosts.com
www.parascope.com
www.philahistorytours.com
www.pirateshouse.com
www.prairieghosts.com
www.privateeyetours.com
www.sanantonioghosts.com
www.sandlapperstours.com
www.savannahghoststours.net
www.savannah.worldweb.com
www.scaryplace.com
www.seelbachhilton.com
www.sfghosthunt.com
www.spanishmilitaryhospital.com
www.seatlepinwsource.com
www.starlinetours.com
www.tbha.org
www.theghostsofsavannah.com
www.theoxfordhotel.com
www.theredlionpub.com
www.theshadowlands.net
www.underground-atlanta.com
www.universalstudios.com
www.ushistory.org
www.viewnews.com
www.visitingdc.com
www.wabashstreetcaves.com
www.wahmee.com
www.washingtonwalks.com
www.whitehouse.gov
www.wrensnest.com

# INDEX